Engaging Multiple Personalities

Clinical Explorations of Dissociative Identity Disorder

Volume 1

Contextual Case Histories

David Yeung

To Olga,

Best wishes, with
appreciation

David Yeung

ISBN *978-1496154217*

BISAC: Psychology / Psychopathology / Dissociative Identity Disorder

Dedication

*My patients all taught me so much,
both about therapy and life itself.*

*This book is dedicated to all those I was able to help and
to those, to my regret, that did not benefit from my efforts.*

Contents

Preface

Cases of Multiple Personality Disorder (MPD), also known as Dissociative Identity Disorder (DID)[1], have always been regarded as rare in mainstream psychiatry. In fact, many mental health professionals have chosen to deny its very existence. News media reports generally include a disclaimer that characterizes it as a controversial diagnosis. This facilitates a dismissal of both the disorder as well as of the individuals afflicted by this condition.

The general public is bewildered and fascinated by DID. Through entertainment media, including books, television and movies, a distorted view of DID is often presented. While it may make for good entertainment, it fails to truly present the depth and intensity of the inherent trauma.

The two volumes in this series are not concerned with proving or disproving the existence of DID. My experience with a few dozen cases in one locale would not pass the vigorous scientific scrutiny required for establishing the clinical validity of any disorder. However, although retired, I remain concerned about the response of psychiatrists if and when a dissociative fragment of

---

[1]Multiple Personality Disorder is the original terminology used in the *Diagnostic and Statistical Manual of Mental Disorders* (DSM). Dissociative Identity Disorder is the new terminology used in the DSM since 1994. In the United States and Canada, the DSM serves as a universal authority for the diagnosis of psychiatric disorders. Treatment recommendations, as well as payments by health care providers, are often determined by DSM classification. For cases histories from before 1994, the old term MPD is used. MPD continues to be the terminology used in the *International Statistical Classification of Diseases and Related Health Problems* (ICD), a medical classification list used by the World Health Organization.

personality appears in the consulting room. I remain concerned about those patients presenting symptoms of depression, panic attacks, substance abuse, bulimia and anorexia who may be frightened to reveal a fragmented mind. Such practical considerations should be the foremost concern of every clinician.

Failure to consider the phenomenon of trauma and dissociation will lead to hopelessly yet tenaciously treating the presenting symptoms while ignoring the underlying problem. It will only prolong a patient's disability and suffering.

If inner conflicts are minimized, DID alters can learn to cooperate like a well-coordinated soccer team; where all the players work together for a common goal. Each member of a soccer team has a particular position, using a specific skill set. This is directly analogous to a cooperating DID system.

Over the course of more than four decades of practicing psychiatry, I acquired some skill in the recognition and treatment of DID. This series documents and distills the clinical experience gained on that journey. It is my hope that it will be of assistance to therapists working with DID so as to improve the care given to patients.

Engaging Multiple Personalities was also written to give confidence to individuals dealing with DID, so that they may gain their own insights to help support the healing process.

The case histories presented here are taken unembellished from my patient files. Nevertheless, I consciously refrained from presenting details that might trigger flashbacks in susceptible readers.

One should always keep in mind that ignoring past trauma simply will not help a patient. Therapists must gently assist the patient in safely engaging in trauma therapy, encouraging this whether or not the patient so wishes. DID patients can successfully engage in and profit from therapy, and by processing the impact of their past traumatic memory, they may reclaim their present.

Finally, when individuals suffering from DID are misdiagnosed, they utilize an extremely disproportionate share of social, health, police and other services. Through these case histories, it is hoped that government authorities will perceive the enormous economic as well as social benefits of the correct diagnosis and treatment of DID.

Warning

If you know or suspect that you have experienced childhood abuse, please make sure you have a good network of support to turn to when exploring such a past. Please stop and ask for help if you feel any emotional turmoil arising when reading this book. While every effort has been made to omit materials that might trigger traumatic memory, the best protection is to have the support of a competent therapist to help process any such turmoil.

Acknowledgments

Ken Smith contributed insights gained from another side of DID; the spousal experience. This perspective further informed and supported the organization of this work. He has also provided various aspects of technical assistance. Sue Anne Cairns offered invaluable help in editing. Finally, my wife Moira, with her extensive experience in writing and editing, has given me much moral support and technical help.

Introduction

Dissociative Identity Disorder is a psychiatric diagnosis included in the DSM 5[2]. It is also included in the ICD 10[3] under the name Multiple Personality Disorder, as used in DSMs published before 1994. These inclusions confirm that experts in the field worldwide regard DID/MPD as a mental health disorder that requires proper diagnosis and treatment.

After graduating from medical school in Hong Kong in the early 1960s, I received further training in psychiatry at preeminent hospitals in London, England. I then came to Canada and practiced psychiatry in a variety of settings: a veterans' hospital, a teaching hospital, an old-fashioned 2,000 patient mental hospital, a short-stay residential crisis intervention facility, a general hospital, and an outpatient clinic. I finally settled into private practice.

In the beginning of my career, despite my education, training, and qualifications, I was ignorant about MPD. Through years of trial and error, I learned to recognize and treat patients with multiple personalities. It was a long and lonely journey of discovery.

I hope that by sharing my clinical experience through this series, new generations of therapists will come to understand the importance of correctly diagnosing DID and treating it appropriately.

Many DID patients display a ubiquitous depression, a thick smoke screen hiding the pathology of trauma and

---

[2]DSM-5 is the 5th edition of the American Psychiatric Association's Diagnostic and Statistical Manual of Mental Disorders.
[3]The ICD 10 is the International Classification of adopted by the World Health Organization.

dissociation.

Once diagnosed as suffering from major depression or other mood disorders, they are quickly given prescriptions for anti-depressant medications. When there is little to no improvement, other anti-depressants are prescribed. Diagnosticians can easily end up characterizing their disorder as "treatment resistant depression." Treatment resistant depression is a misnomer in this context. The depression is not a disease in itself but a symptom of DID. The result is therapeutic failure which is a consequence of attempting to treat the symptom rather than the core pathology. Labelling DID patients with treatment resistant depression leads to chemical based treatments, but DID related depression can indeed be treated. Effective treatment deals with the core issues of past unresolved trauma.

The result is therapeutic failure which is a consequence of attempting to treat the symptom rather than the core pathology. We must not confuse depression as a symptom with depression as the primary disease. Depression can be a normal emotional response to difficult life situations one may encounter. Depression can also be caused by many different illnesses. Finally, it can be a primary mood disorder. Proper treatment requires identifying the nature and cause of the depression. Fixating on eliminating depression while leaving the core pathology untouched does not help the patient.[4]

The heart of DID therapy is engaging the alters on

---

[4]The example of high blood pressure analogously demonstrates the need for correct diagnoses. High blood pressure can be 1) a normal response to physical exertion; 2) Secondary Hypertension due to, for example, disease of the kidney; and 3) Essential Hypertension. They are three entirely different conditions.

their own terms. This is what is detailed in each of the case histories.

I learned far more from my DID patients about identifying and treating the disorder than is ever taught in psychiatric training. It is my sincerest wish to preserve and pass on those insights. I have chosen to do so through the medium of a representative set of their case histories. These case histories are not amalgamations of several patients into one to prove particular points. Each is the actual history of a specific DID patient, taken directly from my notes of patient therapeutic sessions. The only substantive changes are the alteration of personally identifying features in order to protect the privacy of the individual patients.

I do not present only successful cases because the reality is harsh: Treatment was not always successful. However, each patient's case history adds to the collective understanding of the disorder. The presentations of DID differ in every case and, as a result, the therapeutic journey for each has different characteristics.

Each case history demonstrates different methods and approaches to DID therapy in general. They are presented within the case histories in order to show their real-time practical application.

Volume 2 of Engaging Multiple Personalities presents further theoretical and practical guidelines for DID treatment. This includes a presentation of common mistakes and pitfalls in treating dissociative patients, as well as key points to remember in working with the patients. Taken together, it is hoped that they will form the basis of an effective manual for treating DID.

Chapter 1   Joan – The Superwoman

Joan's case illustrates how engaging with alters, the dissociative fragments of personality, is necessary in treatment. The appropriate treatment of this patient led to the return of her previous high social and occupational functioning. While she presented with a classical picture of DID, the appearance of an alter this early in treatment is unusual. The husband's role in the therapy is highly unconventional.

In order to understand the manifestation of Joan's pathology, and the therapeutic approach demanded by it, there are certain classifications of memory that need to be explained. Memory we can easily access is termed explicit memory. This is declarative memory that can be expressed in narrative form. Implicit memory is non-declarative and without verbal representation. It manifests in the body as somatic sensations and visual imageries.

When an experience is encoded in fragmented, non-declarative memory, only raw emotions and physical sensations appear in one's consciousness. These may include hyper-vigilance, sudden and overwhelming feelings of panic or dread. They usually include intense feelings of alienation, rage, and helplessness as well as terror at loss of control.

Instead of precisely expressive words, patients may speak of "wanting to throw up," or a "yucky feeling." Often they have intrusions of bizarre visual images. The patient's inability to translate what is so intensely felt into something expressible in words leaves them frustrated, bewildered, angry, and hopeless. Their dilemma is best expressed by John Harvey (1990) : "Trauma victims have symptoms instead of memories." Working with patients in therapy, a psychiatrist must translate this body of knowledge into appropriate therapeutic processes.

In short, DID is the result of severe childhood trauma. In that sense, it is related to post-traumatic stress disorder (PTSD). Complex PTSD[5] refers to a syndrome in survivors of prolonged and repeated trauma such as incest. Incest also includes a specific element that is common in childhood abuse: the subordination to coercive control. This is different from the experience of victims of PTSD who may have been exposed to a one-time trauma, such as being trapped by an earthquake in a collapsed building. It is not uncommon for DID patients to have alters who suffer from Complex PTSD.

In considering each of the case histories set forth in this book, including Joan's, it is critical to remember the above classifications and the etiology of DID.

Joan's History

Joan was an intelligent and confident entrepreneurial young woman in her 40s, happily married and successful in her business. Her life took a turn for the worse after a motor vehicle accident left her with severe whiplash. This was followed for the next three years by unrelenting pain, depression, anxiety, and severe sleep disturbances. The previously warm outgoing woman was now constantly worried and withdrawn. She had sought help from several conventional and alternative health care practitioners without success.

---

[5]Judith Lewis Herman. Complex PTSD: A Syndrome in Survivors of Prolonged and repeated Trauma. Journal of Traumatic Stress , Vol 5, No.3, 1992. Pages 377-391

One year after the accident, barely hanging on to her work, she came home one evening and abruptly told her husband, a software consultant, that she needed a will. She gave him instructions for the distribution of her assets, and then ran out the door. Chasing her down the stairs all the way to the waterfront, he managed to catch her just as she was jumping into the sea. Clutching her to him so as to prevent another jump, he half-carried, half-dragged her back to their apartment in a high rise building, struggling with her all the way. He had no clue what was going on.

At home, she did not settle down. When Ken, her husband, relaxed his hold on Joan, she lunged for the balcony. He reached out to grab her again. She continued to struggle with him, insisting that she had to jump. He pulled her to the ground and sat on her. While sitting on her, he called Joan's close friend. He told her there was an emergency and demanded that she come at once.

During the 15 minutes before her friend arrived, Joan coolly pointed out to Ken that he would have to fall asleep some time and that as soon as he did, she would get up and jump. When he admitted that he would have to sleep at some point, she agreed to stop struggling: All she had to do was wait until he fell asleep.

As soon as Joan's friend arrived, Ken went to another room and dialed 911. Two police officers came within minutes and took Joan to the hospital. They committed her to the psychiatric ward for observation and treatment. Fortunately, the British Columbia Mental Health Act invests the police with the power to take a person in danger of self-harm to a hospital for assessment by a psychiatrist, even against his or her own wishes.

Joan was taken to a university affiliated teaching

hospital. As the training ground for medical students, interns and residents, teaching hospitals provide a reasonably guaranteed standard of practice. According to her husband, after Joan was escorted into the ambulance and driven to the hospital, she was "knocked out with medication in the psych ward."

Ken's account of the tortuous course that followed illustrates the shortcomings of conventional pharmaceutical-based psychiatry to address the needs of patients such as Joan.

> "The hospital psychiatrist introduced himself and took Joan's family history. He diagnosed Joan as Bipolar Type 2, based on the following information that came from this brief intake interview. She insisted that I be present during the interview. The psychiatrist, in discussing the bipolar diagnosis with me, pointed out the key factors supporting his diagnosis: that she was of Iranian ethnicity, that there was a family history of two uncles with bipolar diagnoses, and that there were addiction issues in one parent and two siblings—one of whom had died as a result of an overdose.
>
> He prescribed medication based on the bipolar diagnosis, despite my strong disagreement. He was confident that the panic Joan had exhibited from 11 pm until 1 am each night was hypomania. I disagreed. It wasn't manic, it was fearful agitation, and I told him so.
>
> After the first 2 days in the hospital, Joan only pretended to swallow the pills given to her by the nursing staff. She spit them out into her hand as soon as the nurse left. When I visited

her, she showed me where she had hidden the pills.

The psychiatrist decided after 4 days that Joan was no longer a danger to herself. Again, I disagreed to no avail.

When Joan was discharged from hospital, she was on medication to lighten the depression. I made sure she was taking the pills for real, but she just seemed to become thicker in mind, foggier.

Joan continued to see the hospital mental health staff. She was extremely frightened of the psychiatrist and insisted that I attend all sessions with her. My presence seemed to reassure her that she would be safe, even though I said nothing. Joan and I met alone with the psychiatrist, with a resident he was training, and sometimes with both of them together.

The sole therapy was treatment by medication. There was no other approach used or offered for consideration. Joan became increasingly unhappy and physically uncomfortable on the medication. Nevertheless, she gave it a try and stayed on it for several months. The suicidal ideation did not stop. Several more attempts were made, although usually not as dramatic as that first evening.

Six months after discharge from the hospital, Joan went to a psychologist who specialized in PTSD. She felt comfortable enough to be alone with the therapist for most sessions. While these sessions helped a bit, every time any internal pressures were released, Joan immediately took on additional burdens both worldly and emotional. The result was that the decompression was immediately reversed. Again, there seemed no genuine benefit that lasted even overnight.

Throughout this time, she was in pain. The trigger points that often indicate chronic fatigue were hyper-sensitive. The psychologist, after consultation with her PTSD mentor, felt that Joan had experienced substantial abuse in the past but was too fragile to approach it yet. She worked with this psychologist for 3 months.

The suicide attempts during this period arose very quickly. They usually involved Joan attempting to jump out of the car when it was moving. These were always preceded by a sudden upheaval of anger, and a statement that she wanted it all to be over. I became adept at slowing down and pulling to the side of the road while clutching Joan with my right hand as she opened the passenger door, undid the seat belt and fought to jump out.

Because the pain re-occurred within hours of a therapeutic massage, Joan tried cranio-sacral therapy[6]. Again, at her request, I remained in the room during these sessions. While Joan was

---

[6]A number of my patients had childhood abuse memories surface after hands-on therapy; such as massage, chiropractic and cranio-sacral therapy.

in the washroom just before starting the third session, the cranio-sacral therapist told me that she thought there were going to be memories of abuse coming up that day. She said could feel it in Joan's body.

When the session commenced, horrific images arose in Joan's mind, terrifying her. This went on for over an hour. The therapist encouraged her to express what she was seeing. She settled down somewhat by the end of the session, but everyone was rattled by both the content and vividness of the images. After a few more sessions, it was clear that the ongoing arising of these images was not helpful. Joan was unable to process them in a way that made her feel any safer. She was too afraid of the images to return again.

Throughout this 4 month period, there were continuing suicidal ideation and periodic attempts, along with her occasional disappearances for hours at a time."

At this point that Joan was referred to me by her family doctor.

The interval between the motor vehicle accident and seeing me was about three and a half years. Joan had consulted a total of nine doctors in this intervening time, mainly for her whiplash pain.

First Session: The Woman and the Child

Joan arrived at my office as a smartly dressed professional woman. She seemed morose and fearful, and insisted on her husband accompanying her for this first interview.

Rather than sitting facing me, she slumped back on the couch. She asked her husband to speak about her background and current circumstances. He gave the above summary, which Joan then timidly confirmed. With her eyes closed, she spoke in a whispery, child-like voice. She told me that she was afraid of going insane. She felt the recurrent images of abuse and accompanying mental aberrations were signs of that insanity.

Joan was born overseas and came to Canada at infancy. Raised primarily by her grandmother, she remembered her father as a physically abusive alcoholic. He had been born rich and had a business, but did not need to work for the money. Her father had died when Joan was twenty, and her mother was living by herself in another city. She was not close to her mother. Joan had been married before. A teenage son was living with her and her husband of six years. She had two university degrees and was successfully engaged in a highly competitive business enterprise.

Her symptoms included depression and disturbances in sleep pattern. These had been ongoing since the car accident. Joan was afraid of going to sleep. When going to bed, she experienced initial insomnia, followed by a restless sleep. She was sleeping primarily from early morning to very late morning and sometimes into the early afternoon.

On further inquiry, Joan said, "I have to be vigilant. If I fall asleep, I will not be ready for the next accident. I cannot live my life like this." She gave the impression of being hyper-vigilant; feeling unsafe and vulnerable yet always bracing herself for the next accident.

She was bothered by nightmares and recurring intrusive imagery of being sexually abused. Her major concern was feeling overwhelmed by these images. She could not accept them as memory but was willing to accept them as signs of possible insanity. She was prescribed Remeron (a sleeping medication), Epivol (a mood stabilizer), and Celebrex (for whiplash pain).

Joan's story strongly suggested a case of childhood abuse, and I suspected that Joan was likely in a state of dissociation.

I gave Joan my assessment that she was not going insane but that she was likely recalling some bad experiences from her past. Although the details she remembered might not be completely accurate, she was neither hallucinating nor having delusions. I told her that certain things were clear to me: "Bad things happened to you as a child. They happened a long time ago. The important thing is to learn that right here, right now, you are safe."

I told her that she did not have to tell me everything she remembered, and that remembering everything exactly was not necessary. I reiterated that the most important thing was to learn that she was safe in the present. The person I was addressing appeared to have the mental state of a four or five year old child. While a child that age might not have understood what I was saying on a cognitive level, the tone of my voice calmed Joan down.

Like other traumatized individuals who suffer with terrifying memories and bodily sensations, Joan had a hard time being in the present. She was continually being drawn into the past to re-experience early traumas over and over again. As a result, she was perpetually subject to uncontrollable irresistible emotional flashbacks. Joan needed to learn how to experience and hold on to a feeling of safety in the present moment, rather than repeatedly becoming overwhelmed by traumatic memories.

After asking a few more questions, I assured her and her husband that she was not suffering from bipolar affective disorder and did not need mood stabilizers. However, I gave her a sample package of the tranquilizer Zyprexa. I suggested that she keep it available as a small dose might give her and her husband a brief respite should the intrusion of memories become too intense. My recommendation was that only half a dose would be needed, and then only when the memories seemed momentarily unbearable.

As is common in many patients with abuse experience, Joan had lost the ability to feel safe. She had lost even the memory of what safety felt like. It seemed clear that the unwelcome and recurring images were linked to past abuse. The challenge was to help her acknowledge, work through, and resolve past traumas without re-traumatizing her. Over the next three years, I helped her learn that not only was she safe right then in my office with her husband beside her, but also that she could carry that sense of safety outside my office into her everyday world.

Some psychiatrists might question whether addressing the apparently four or five year old child that presented in my office would encourage the patient to remain in a regressed position. In terms of safety and establishing a therapeutic alliance for healing, my experience taught me that the best way to access traumatic memory would be to listen to this voice, whether it was presenting as a regressed child or as a DID alter.

In fact, Joan was suffering from Complex PTSD; characterized by fight or flight physiological arousal and triggered by the intrusion of traumatic memories. She also exhibited long periods of immobility some mornings, complaining that she could move neither her fingers nor limbs.[7]

Unlike ordinary memories, highly charged traumatic experiences excite a physiological reaction, one that has been cultivated by evolution through learning by surviving the high-stress environments that characterized human existence. Early traumatic experiences do not simply leave behind cognitive memories that can be switched on and off like a TV show. They remain trapped in the body.

Biologically, the early traumatic experience agitates the neurochemical activity centers of the brain that affect memory encoding and recollection. When the traumatic memories and body-states associated with them return, an individual is truly re-living the experience of trauma through their body. Because their body is reacting right now, they do not experience that the trauma belongs to the past. The patient often appears to be frozen with fear. They have an avoidance reaction, wanting to shrink away.

I had to consider what Joan's appearance as a frightened four or five year old child indicated. Perhaps it

---

[7]Peter Levine presents an ethological model of the fight/flight/freeze responses seen when animals encounter life-threatening situations. Levine, P. Waking the Tiger: Healing Trauma through the Body. North Atlantic Books, 1997.

was regression, or perhaps it was an alter who spoke, acted, and thought like a child. Whether or not Joan had DID would become apparent in future sessions. As yet, there was no basis nor need to make a firm diagnosis.

Second Session: The Secret Watcher

I recognized Joan's decision to return to me for a second session was courageous. It must have seemed risky to her. From her perspective, it would either open the floodgates to a painful past she did not want to believe or result in her being declared insane and locked up in an institution.

Once again she came in with her husband. She insisted that he stay, and leaned away from me on the chair. With her eyes half-closed, she whimpered like a frightened child.

Traumatized people, especially victims of childhood abuse, require much reassurance. After thanking her for returning to see me, I commented that she was very brave to do so. I again reassured her that I did not want her to recall and relive her entire past trauma in our sessions. I emphasized that while I believed she was on the verge of remembering, being trapped in the past was causing unnecessary distress in the present. It was interfering with her life, and that interference was what we needed to work on.

Joan curled up in the chair. She rubbed her head at the temple, and said that her eye hurt. After a short pause, a suddenly defiant Joan straightened up, glared at me, and announced that she didn't think I knew anything at all.

The timid child-like Joan had disappeared. In her place was someone with a completely different posture, affect and speech pattern. I felt a shiver up my spine, as I always did when an alter first appeared on the scene.

I asked, "Who's saying that?"

She answered huffily, "I am not going to tell."

I asked, "You are not Joan, are you?"

Joan nodded her head emphatically in agreement.

"I'd like to know your name, because you are obviously important. Is there a name I can call you, such as Anne or Betty?"

The immediate response was a sneer, "That shows that you don't know nothing!" She folded her hands across her chest.

"Why are you saying that?"

"I am a boy! You don't even know, you stupid man!"

This abrupt appearance of a "boy" was as dramatic an alter's entrance into a therapy session as I had ever experienced. I had no trouble identifying this "boy" as a dissociated part of the ego.

Alters usually appear in much later sessions, rarely as early as in the second one. Why had this alter presented itself so early? Had I inadvertently done something to create this alter by suggesting or inducing this display of bravado in a frightened and vulnerable woman? I believe the steadying presence of her husband beside her, and my calm reassurances, allowed Joan to feel safe enough to reveal this innermost secret to both of us simultaneously.

I then said, "What, may I ask, is your name?"

He said, "I have no name."

"What is your job? You must be serving a purpose being here with Joan."

The boy understood and answered without hesitation, "I am the secret watcher. It is my job to make sure no one is lying."

"Can I call you Secret Watcher then?"

He didn't like that, so I suggested SW. He said that would be OK. I then spoke with SW for a while.

I asked him how old he was, and he answered five. I asked if there were others inside. He said yes while making a face indicating that it was another completely stupid question.

SW then said he was the bravest one of them all, and that he was not afraid to come out. He said no one knew this, but he was the one who loved to run around and to play cowboys and Indians when Joan was a child. He said that everyone thought Joan was a tomboy, but she wasn't - it was actually SW. He said that whenever a grown-up would get angry for something he did, like hitting someone or knocking over a vase, he would disappear and leave Joan holding the bag. He said that he didn't trust grown-ups.

I asked SW if he trusted Ken, gesturing toward Joan's husband. SW immediately answered with a big "No! Ken hates little boys."

I asked, "What about me?" SW might be five, but I got a measured adult-style response as he took his time, saying, "I have to wait and see."

Then, as abruptly as he had appeared, he said he had to go, that he was tired...and he was gone.

Joan slid back deep into the chair and closed her eyes for about 30 seconds. Then she shifted, opened her eyes and said in her timid voice that she had to go to the washroom. As she exited the office, her husband and I looked speechlessly at each other. After a few moments, I asked Ken if he thought I had done anything, directly or indirectly, to suggest the existence of an alter to Joan. He confirmed that I had not.

When SW appeared, my thought was that the most important thing to do was to keep still, to maintain a sense of warm space so as to allow whatever was to happen, to happen without judgment. Questioning SW's appearance, or saying anything that might be interpreted as an attack or disbelief, would have been a mistake.

Up to that point, I had only spent one hour with Joan - in the first session a few days before. There were some puzzling questions. In particular, there was the question as to why the alter SW had never shown himself to the doctors and nurses in the psychiatric ward of the hospital, nor to any of the other mental health professionals Joan had seen.

Many factors influence whether an alter will appear on the scene. It could be something in the environment, perhaps a triggering word or some other cue, as in Leila's case history described later in Chapter 4.

It was clear that SW had done his job of assessing me. Perhaps he had decided to reveal himself to me because I set up a safe space and Ken was there as an external protector of Joan. This confluence of circumstances established enough of a sense of security that Joan's DID system could risk revealing this innermost secret.

I always assumed that my patients could read me, or any other psychiatrist, like a book. Openness and respectful curiosity shown in the interview process helps to foster a stronger therapeutic alliance than would be possible in a hospital psychiatric ward. Such wards may appear unsafe to patients, with ever-changing staff working different shifts.[8]

SW's initiative in coming out and speaking with me seemed to signal that the DID system of host and alters deemed it safe for me to meet SW. In this way, I was offered the opportunity to communicate with the system directly. While an alter's perspective may reflect their emotional development or perhaps the age when they split off, it does not necessarily reflect their intellectual capacity.

Consider the possibility that instead of engaging SW directly, I had suggested that Joan snap out of it in some way and stop pretending to be a boy. Some psychiatrists might construe that alternative as a necessary wake-up call to a patient. In fact, that kind of impatience would close the gate to the most important source of information from and for the patient; the alters. They are the holders of memories that the host personality does not know and cannot yet access.

When Joan returned from the washroom, she sank

---

[8]The exception would be a specialized Dissociation Unit, such as the one run by Dr. Colin Ross in Winnipeg, Manitoba years ago. Colin Ross and Frank Putnam are pioneers in the field of DID. Each published a textbook on DID in 1989.

into the chair once again, sighing with what looked like great fatigue. I asked her how she was feeling and she replied that she was completely worn out. I asked if she remembered what we had been talking about during the last 20 minutes. She said no, that the session felt very foggy and she really couldn't remember any of it. I gently told her that a little boy had been here, that he had said a few things, that he called himself the Secret Watcher, and that I had a good chat with him. Joan remained silent and thoughtful.

Because I knew I was seeing a genuine DID, I presumed there were other alters inside. I said that everyone inside could hear us talking, that I wanted them all to know that I cared about each of them, and that I wanted to teach them how to feel safe. I learned later, from her husband, that she had checked with him after leaving my office to see if there really had been a little boy that came out.

It must have been quite a shock for Joan to learn that there was a little boy inside who had ventured out to speak to me. Yet, I did not want to hide the presence of the Secret Watcher from her. I believed it was time that they get acquainted with each other. The first step toward healing and becoming whole is to dissolve the amnestic barrier separating fragmented identities from each other.

Initial Treatment Plan

I would learn that many of Joan's alters had severe PTSD symptoms. She suffered from flashbacks, mostly at night. Therefore, I concentrated on ways for her to process her trauma memory. As with many DID patients, the predominant problem was hyper-vigilance and severe flashbacks associated with PTSD.

During the initial period, I considered therapeutic techniques including hypnosis, EFT and/or EMDR.[9] These techniques can sometimes be used to loosen up the pathological coupling between some alters, the traumatic memories they hold, and the physiological arousal associated with those memories.

Most of the alters were just too young for me to employ these techniques. Eventually, I found that the most appropriate approach for Joan was to just talk to the alters, and work with what arose on an ad hoc basis. I let the system decide, in its internally assessed order of urgency, who and what needed to be dealt with during each session.

I met with Joan weekly for two-hour sessions. The focus was on Joan learning to be stable and feel safe. My motto was to go slow. Going slow is key to limiting the risk of re-traumatization. I stressed to the system that every alter was important and was to be respected. Many came out, both in my office and in the evening engaging with Ken, Joan's husband.

---

[9]DID patients score high in hypnotizability. There is much written on the use of hypnosis in the treatment of DID. Working knowledge of and experience in hypnosis is an asset for a DID therapist. Use of hypnosis, whether in a formal or informal way, is useful in leading the patient to the safety of the "now." Applying hypnosis in that way, rather than using it to explore the past, is key to avoiding re-traumatization as well as maintaining the safety of the session environment.

Emotional Freedom Technique (EFT) and Eye Movement Desensitization and Reprocessing (EMDR) are techniques to affect the emotional component of a mental content through re-processing.

Problems Related to Multiplicity

After SW appeared in my office and spoke to me in Ken's presence, other alters, as well as SW, began to come out regularly each evening at home. Their appearance was an expression of trust and confidence by the system. Their appearances, however, were intense and difficult as they were accompanied by their unprocessed trauma. It was surely not advisable to instruct Ken to ignore these alters, which would convey invalidation and rejection.

To establish a therapeutic alliance with traumatized alters is necessary, but to do so one must appreciate that they remain hidden based on the fear that they will not be acknowledged. Even worse is the fear that the memories they hold will be denied and dismissed. This fear is ingrained by abusers, who always impress upon the victimized child that no one will believe them. While it was certainly quite unnerving to both Joan and Ken to see what used to be hidden, Ken learned to respond appropriately to these alters.

Each alter may have its own opinions, which are often at odds with the opinions of other alters and the host. As one might expect, there was much conflict among the alters in Joan's inner world. Daily functioning got bogged down because of disagreements. Once activated, presumably as a result of the pain triggered by the motor vehicle accident, Joan's inner world became chaotic. It was as if the alters were engaged in a civil war. Sometimes one alter would have a murderous rage toward another. At other times, one alter would be happy to destroy everyone inside. Often, a suicidal alter felt that killing herself would be best for everyone inside as well as Ken, her son, and everyone else she knew.

The alters also had very different feelings about significant people involved in Joan's life. Some alters were attached to and loved Ken. Others were angry with and critical of him for a variety of reasons. Some were enraged at Joan's son and wished him gone.

The husband met with different alters for a couple of hours or more every evening. Many alters came out simply to be acknowledged. One was an 80 year old man who enjoyed meditation and chanting. Another was a 40 year old man who drank alcohol and could erupt in violence, sometimes slapping Joan. There were three sisters, very old, who remembered past events and kept them for Joan. They served as a specific memory bank.

I did not go into detail with or about these alters. I only intervened with alters who presented problems for Joan or when they presented themselves in my office. I presumed all of them once served, or were still serving, some important functions for the system.

During my time with Joan, she was examined by a psychiatrist doing an assessment for the insurance claim relating to the motor vehicle accident. This doctor did not believe that Joan was in pain or had any negative psychological impact from the accident.

It is instructive to note that he completely missed the appearance of a child alter during his assessment. He had asked Joan to do the serial seven test, counting backwards from 100 by subtracting 7 sequentially; 100, 93, 86 etc. Ken, waiting by the door, reported that Joan held up her fingers and counted backwards on them. When Joan did that, the psychiatrist raised his voice, telling her to stop acting like a child.

The alter known as the Avenger had a fierce reaction

to this insurance assessment: She felt betrayed that Joan was not believed. The Avenger railed, "I want that doctor's family to suffer." When the insurance company settled the case, the avenger remained enraged. The Avenger blamed Ken for "letting evil people get off scot-free." The evil person in this case referred to the assessment psychiatrist. By default, the husband had to handle this alter when she came out at night. During our office sessions, I was kept busy working with other alters on their issues. I did not meet the Avenger directly.

Problems Related to Traumatic Memory Upheaval

Once therapy commenced, Joan began experiencing bodily pain totally unrelated to the car accident. The pain seemed far more connected to physical and sexual abuse of the past. Rather than being localized where the whiplash had caused soft tissue injury or at the chronic fatigue syndrome trigger points, she experienced pain in the pubic area as well as in the vagina. Joan developed a skin lesion on her forehead that remained open as a result of incessant scratching. The back and shoulder pain was never mentioned in our sessions.

The husband was kept busy dealing with alters coming out and reliving the traumatic past, generally from 11pm to 2am. According to one of the alters, this was the time when the abuse had repeatedly occurred. On occasion, Joan realized that the terror and pain in a nightmare was not a dream but a piece of memory concerning an actual event of the past. After an exhausting session in my office, Joan was often "confused" for the rest of the day.

One vigilant alter stirred up after a session with me insisted that his/her function was to be watchful. This was not SW being watchful to evaluate the trustworthiness of people. This alter's role was to prevent Joan from falling sleep until after Ken was snoring. This was the first time there was a direct explanation for why she always waited for Ken to fall asleep before she would close her eyes.

Following most sessions, but particularly in the first several months, Joan wanted to walk outside. Ken would park the car and they would walk by the ocean. Joan would invariably slow down, complain of a pain in the temple behind her right eye, and then an alter would pop out in fury, enraged at Ken. After expressing that rage, the alter would often say they were tired and had to leave now. As soon as they said that, they would be gone. Joan would then re-appear, always somewhat dazed. The alters that emerged during those walks were never the alters that I had engaged in the session. The process of therapy was clearly not confined to the office sessions.

The fact that Ken was present during the office sessions without challenging the alters, coupled with the activating quality of the therapy, created the opportunity for the alters to express themselves directly afterwards. The walks appeared to be another opportunity, following her end-of-session naps, for Joan to further consolidate therapeutic gains. The alters continued to feel confident in coming out to engage without smoke-screens as Ken understood that his role was simply to listen and witness – not to defend himself.

Joan began to remember more and more of the abuse, which was always extremely violent. The memories came spontaneously. I continued to stick to another of the guidelines I had long ago established in my work with DID patients: Never ask the patient to elaborate on their trauma history. There are two main reasons for this, the first being to avoid re-traumatization. The second is that overenthusiastic pursuit of detail by the therapist might encourage the formation of false memory in a highly suggestible patient who unconsciously is trying to please the therapist.

I introduced a "5% rule" to Joan. I suggested that an alter should limit their experience of the pain to 5% of the actual memory of pain, and in that way avoid being overwhelmed by it. 5% seemed to work because it gave a boundary of tolerability, regardless of that boundary's illusory nature. This was a highly suggestive instruction. The notion of 5% simply acted as a conceptual framework to enable the pain to be rationed out in a controllable fashion. Within that conceptual framework, if the emotions were too intense, I was able to encourage limiting the pain to 2% of its original intensity. This further instruction was successfully used to limit the impact of the recollection of the trauma to a manageable level.

The trauma was extraordinarily powerful. Time, even four decades, did not seem to dilute its intensity. Nevertheless, every little technique helped.

Problems outside the Therapy Sessions

Day-to-day reality was filled with obstacles for Joan. Numerous distractions interrupted the flow of therapy. Her teenage son was acting out, an unavoidable circumstance given the tumultuous rocky last several years in the family coupled with the ordinary growing pains of a teenager. Ken managed to keep her business going while she maintained a small measure of engagement.

At night, Ken encountered numerous alters, some violently angry, and others who were simply terrified. Suicidal threats were constant in the initial phase. These slowly simmered down. SW became mellower, and his anger toward the husband diminished. It turned out that SW had more conflicts with the teenage son than the husband. Many new alters kept coming out to be acknowledged.

After the alters would have their say each night with Ken, he reminded them to focus on the safety of the present, reinforcing what I was teaching in the office sessions. Joan was then able to fall asleep quite quickly, often before Ken and without medication. She began to have a sense of regaining control during the day. She also re-established direct contact with her business.

Healing Rituals in the Office

In our weekly meetings, Joan insisted that her husband always sit with us in my office. At first, I was tentative in my acceptance of this condition. Over time, I found that I needed him to help "translate" her slurred mumblings. He was also needed to report on the late night appearances of alters. For the next three and half years, with the exception of two sessions when he was unavoidably out of town, Joan did therapy in my office with her husband present. Therapy was almost always conducted with alters.

We quickly established a routine. Joan would arrive in my office and slide into two chairs that I had pushed together to form a cot-like enclosure. She lay there with her eyes closed. Her feet were tucked beneath her with a blanket covering her legs. This physical setup was the result of my attempt to make her feel comfortable. It evolved from her wishes, rather than my direction. I simply followed her lead in terms of how she indicated she might be comfortable.

Unless SW or some of the other angry alters came out to talk, Joan always curled up on the chairs. After asking her permission, Ken would then give his report on the last week's late night conversations with different alters, reading from his concurrently taken notes. She would occasionally interject, making comments to ensure that he was communicating the conversations with accuracy.

Ken always finished by asking Joan if the notes were now completely accurate. This ensured that she understood that she was in control of what was communicated and that it was indeed being heard. This also meant that at no time could he interject his own commentary. His role was limited to being the recorder. There was no defending himself, and no contextual explanation for whatever the alter might feel angry with him about. In effect, this was key to maintaining the safety and integrity of the sessions: They were for Joan's healing, not joint marriage counseling.

Very early on, Joan began a ritual of rubbing her temple or touching her eyes, which indicated the imminent entrance of an alter. A few alters needed individual therapy. Each of these had a special function connected with a traumatic experience that needed processing. Drawing from the material reported by Joan's husband, I approached only those alters whose words had been read to me. The alters would comment, confirm, or amend these reports. I then worked with each on the particular issues they introduced. I usually worked with two to three alters in each session.

I explained to Joan and, in fact to all the alters, that together they made up a system. I pointed out that the system, operating on hyper-alert, had protected Joan for many years when she was in continual danger. It was time for the system to reassess Joan's new environment, which was very different from the environment of the past. The alters did not need to hide from one another any longer, nor did they need to be perpetually on hyper-alert. Now it was time for everyone to work together as a team. It was time for them to begin sharing and communicating.

I also told her that in order to heal, she needed to approach her therapy like a soccer team in training for the World Cup. Without that intensity of focus on the goal of healing, the difficulties would continue. I stressed that I knew that all the alters could hear what I was saying, even if they weren't out and talking. I reiterated that I cared about each of them, and appreciated how they had, in their own ways, all helped the system survive. I reminded them that even though they didn't need to be on hyper-alert, their concerns and insights were still important.

Joan invariably fell asleep for about 15 minutes at the end of each session. Her husband and I would retreat to another room, have some coffee and discuss what had happened during the session or at home, and plan for future intervention. This ritual always ended with her getting up and going to the washroom. At that juncture, her husband and I would go back to my office and wait for her return.

I believe that sleeping by herself in the office gave Joan time to consolidate what she had learned in the session. I had purposely created a space in my office where she could safely rest, curled up and wrapped in a blanket. This allowed Joan to metabolize past trauma by actively translating a verbal message of safety into physical and literal terms.

This choice of hers to sleep, knowing that a close caring person (in this case, Ken) would be there to protect her if necessary, gave her the experience of receiving the soothing comfort that any injured child seeks. Being left alone in apparent inactivity was highly therapeutic for Joan, enabling a gentle transition from the intense experience of therapy with the alters to re-emergence into the outside world. This ritual was helping Joan learn to overcome the bodily distress and triggers of the PTSD symptoms.

Husband as Quasi-Therapist

Some of the most difficult and significant healing happened between formal office sessions, when Joan was at home with her husband. By accompanying her in the sessions at my office, this intuitive spouse quickly learned how to facilitate healing. I asked him to be receptive to the alters, to acknowledge their presence and ask simple questions about their names, ages, and what their roles were in the system. Many alters appeared and were acknowledged – expressing both their pain and intense need for comforting. Some only made one or two appearances.

I have found that partners who stay with a DID patient without exploiting their vulnerability are usually kind, caring, and understanding. While the therapist cannot give the patient more than one or two hours per week, the partner as quasi-therapist has the potential to offer many hours per week of attention to the alters to help resolve their PTSD. With some help from the therapist, a partner who engages directly and appropriately with alters can be a major support as an active healing partner. Most importantly, partners have the capacity to physically comfort the patient through non-sexual intimacy and touch. That is the best way to comfort a patient, just as one would comfort a child. However, it is not something a therapist can do.

Complications may arise as mixing the roles of husband and therapist can be risky. I am still pondering whether designating the spouse as quasi-therapist at home can be a practice generalized to other patients. This was the only instance in my experience that a spouse, by default, functioned as an in-house quasi-therapist. In that role, he did much of the most intense therapy required for healing Joan. The situation was unavoidable since alters started to come out at night in that atmosphere of genuine love and kindness.

The Flow of Therapy

In one census that her husband recorded, the total number of alters inside Joan was 39. However, in the office sessions I engaged only the limited number of alters who needed my help. Although I assume that all alters are there for a reason, perhaps something as simple as balancing power in the system, alters who are not causing problems can be left alone in therapy. I focused on teaching those alters who were most frightened, or most interfering with functioning, to live appropriately in the here and now, cooperating with the other alters. This job, requiring sensitivity and patience, is more complex than it may sound.

Fear of danger is a tenacious obstacle for traumatized people to overcome. They must practice reconnecting to the safety of the present moment, learning over and over again that nothing bad happens when they let down their hyper-vigilant guard a bit. At the same time, the function of the alters, when not out of balance, needs to be appreciated and sustained to ensure that if danger does arise, the alters' protective qualities can be immediately accessed. The purpose is to establish a level of vigilance appropriate to the present situation, rather than the hyper-vigilance tied to past trauma.

Some of the protective qualities of the alters were demonstrated quite clearly by SW. In addition to his charge as the Secret Watcher, evaluating the safety of people the host encountered, he had also served as an active protector. In the midst of some of the early childhood abuse, he successfully stopped it by forcing Joan to repeatedly knock her head against the floor. In that way, he frightened the abuser. SW had figured out that the abuser wanted to avoid dealing with hospitals, police or other authorities. Smashing Joan's head was a way that he could scare the abuser into stopping: A hospitalized Joan might draw the authorities' attention to the abuse.

Therapeutic conversation should be appropriate for the age of the alters. With the alter known as Julie, I was talking to a four year old in simple kindergarten language. I held her hand gently, speaking softly until she got the message. All the time, I knew that Julie was a part of an otherwise worldly, sophisticated, successful entrepreneur with two university degrees. Ken's presence reassured her that the physical holding of the hand could not be misinterpreted.

While repeatedly reassuring the very young Julie that all the pain was indeed in the past, I kept calling her to the present, in a very simple, concrete way fitting for her age. I asked her to look outside the office window where she could see a local landmark and taught her the geographic reality: My office was thousands of miles away from where the abuse had occurred. Reminding her of the current date reinforced that the present was many decades away from when she experienced the abuse. I encouraged her to recognize that the abuser was no longer around. Therefore, right now, she was safe from him.

Establishing a safe environment and giving lessons for processing trauma in that safe environment combined, over time, in a potent positive way. In the beginning however, while rocking and scratching herself wildly at night, Julie relived powerful traumatic experiences. She was trapped in the repeating physiological and psychological arousal of trauma. It seemed as if these patterns were so deeply ingrained and went so far back, that it would be difficult for her to escape their hold. Session after session, over and over, I repeated my reassurances that the past was the past, and now we could come to the here and now, today, in this light, in this room, in this city. Many nights, living in a world of four decades earlier, Julie scratched herself so fiercely that she drew blood.

When she was reliving the abuse experiences as body memory, Julie also rocked herself in a sitting position for lengthy intervals at home. Joan's resourceful husband was able to improvise unique ways of comforting her that I could not use in my role as her psychiatrist; such as lying in bed with her, keeping a pillow between them.

He was able to help alters calm down by putting Joan's head on his chest so that they could hear his steady heartbeat. Sometimes the focus was for the alters to feel the up and down rhythm of his chest as he breathed calmly. These often enabled the alter that was out and in distress to slow down their own physiological response. In that way, the alter was able to learn physically what it was to feel safe once again. Clearly, the psychiatrist cannot employ that level of body-based calming strategies.

There was no need to focus on the details of the abuse beyond working with the flashbacks presented. I concentrated on empowering Julie to stay with the present. What mattered was how she felt now, decades after the original traumatic experiences. I made it clear that any alters who wanted to tell me something were welcome to do so.

By acting as a moderator when the alters were telling me their stories, I was able to protect them from re-traumatization. I would stop them when I felt it was necessary, saying it was enough for the day. I would redirect them to the here and now, bringing their attention to the landmark bridge visible through my office window or to their own breathing.

During the ensuing sessions, different alters came out, many in the office but most of them at home. Of the 39 alters the husband counted, 27 of them made themselves known in the first six months of therapy. The colorful household group included several who were between three and ten years old, a few infants, several in their 20s, and, of course, the elderly man and women mentioned earlier.

While most of these alters were handled by Ken, I concentrated on the seven or eight who were the most highly active in the system. Through listening and providing understanding, support and comfort, I was able to correct some cognitive errors without frightening them or denying their insights. Over and over, I called them back into the current reality.

All the alters carried extreme emotions, but at this point in Joan's life there were a few that seemed to be creating more harm than benefit in their function. For example, one alter never felt financially secure, adamantly insisting that she was perpetually under the threat of crushing poverty. Knowing that her business was reasonably successful, I asked her what amount of money she felt was necessary for safety. She said she would need $35 million cash in the bank before she could even start to feel safe. Ken pointed out later to me that this amounted to about $1,000,000 per alter.

The general outcome was that as the alters' emotional intensity lessened, their sharp edges smoothed with time and the hard definiteness of their characters was softened. Nevertheless, they retained the functions for which they were created: the paranoid continued to exercise caution and watchfulness while the depressed guarded against careless over-enthusiasm. Both groups became more realistic and more able to withstand the ordinary ups and downs of life. The harsh punitive one became the organizer; maintaining discipline while no longer feeling compelled to torment and destroy those alters she considered weak.

Because of his energy, courage and inner strength, SW was a highly valuable resource. He was the one who knew, or knew of, most of the other alters. He was sometimes able to provide early warnings about some of the most fragile alters who were in danger of collapse from their memories and pain.

SW was quite a character. He liked fast cars and fried chicken. He would be outspoken and angry at times, and took an active role bringing out other parts for therapy. He certainly had language skills and understanding far beyond the age of five, but insisted that he was unable to write anything down in a journal because he was too young. It was a joy to watch the mellowing of his attitude toward Ken and me. Gradually he became less mistrustful, less cynical, and even seemed to lose the need to present as a sharply distinct individual.

Conclusion of Therapy

Once Joan started therapy, her depression slowly but somewhat steadily dissipated. Within the first few months, the suicidal ideation become far less pronounced. Suicide attempts diminished in number as well as intensity. It was clear that the correct therapy was having a substantial, rapid, and positive impact. Nevertheless, sometimes sparked by a TV documentary or movie, crises arose and were still able to gather momentum.

I was spending far more time with her husband and her alters than with Joan's host personality, the businesswoman who never needed any help from me. When I had an opportunity to speak to the host at the conclusion of therapy, I found her articulate, well-informed, and brilliant. A year after concluding therapy with me, Joan represented Canada at international conferences held in Europe.

With the help of her spouse, she gradually eased back to work soon after she started coming to see me.

Before the end of treatment, she had already returned to a high social/occupational functioning. The inner conglomeration behaved, usually, like a reasonably efficient corporation. It set up some rules for the child-alters: they had to stay out of the workplace, but they could come out in the evening to play or make a mess in the house. At work, there was the occasionally necessary appearance of an assertive alter who took charge in an appropriately definite way. Her colleagues did not seem to see this alter as strange, but were impressed by her energy and organizational efficiency. By the conclusion of therapy, Joan was working full time.

Years Later

Six years after my retirement, I ran into Joan and her husband near her office. We exchanged simple pleasantries. She was charming and appeared happy to see me. Her business enterprise was flourishing. Her husband looked happy and at ease.

Later, her husband was able to meet with me and, with Joan's explicit permission, fill me in on how she had fared in the intervening years. Her inner world, ruptured from terrible early trauma, could not be completely healed in our time together. However, if high social functioning indicated improved mental health, Joan's progress was indeed amazing. Making the correct diagnosis and applying the correct therapy was the key to this outcome. Her pathological depression was eliminated through treatment of the core trauma with psychotherapy.

This case clearly illustrates how attentive and patient engagement with the alters, who hold traumatic memories, helps DID patients to process the trauma. If attention was focused solely on the depression or whiplash pain, which were smoke screens of sorts, Joan would never have gotten better. I was deeply gratified to discover she had come to enjoy a good quality of life in her marriage, her profession, and her travels to foreign countries for business and leisure.

Some may question whether the effective management of alters is a true healing. I am confident that psychotherapy helped Joan through some of the most turbulent times in her adult life, enabling her to move beyond the pain, depression, and disability.

Therapeutic Keys

It is interesting to note that in this patient, whiplash pain was the presenting physical complaint that appeared to be at the crux of her depression. This is what had led her to seek help from multiple conventional and alternative treatments. She never complained of this physical pain during the entire course of her treatment with me. The pain she complained of during our sessions was clearly tied to abuse.

The fact that the whiplash resulted from an accident that was third party verifiable seemed to fulfill Joan's need to express pain that would be acknowledged. One might reasonably presume that by engaging the alters who held the body memories of the pain of abuse directly, the whiplash related pain was no longer needed to be an ostensible basis for the host's difficulties. Once the alters understood that they were being listened to, respected, and valued, there was no need to have verifiable present pain as an excuse for seeking help.

The spouse's participation is an outstanding feature of this case. While it was extremely positive for Joan, one cannot presume that all spouses or partners of DID patients will have that level of stability or kindness. The therapist must consider the positive and negative qualities of the spouse/partner in making recommendations for support outside the office session process.

Chapter 2 General Introduction to Dissociation and Multiple Personality Disorder

The term dissociation has been used since the late 1800s to cover a range of psychological functions from normal to pathological, from functional to organic, and for both descriptive and explanatory purposes. The concept of dissociation causes disagreement in academic circles because its meaning is seen as ambiguous and problematic. In part, this is because dissociation arises across a spectrum of intensity, from simply daydreaming to the pathology known as Dissociative Identity Disorder.[10]

The Experience of Dissociation

Dissociation is when we deviate from our usual patterns in memory, identity, perception and/or consciousness. It is not rare. Simple experiences of dissociation often occur when one is bored or caught in a temporarily frustrating life situation. For example, people often fall into a trance-like state while driving on the highway and pass by their exit without any awareness of doing so. Similarly, one may gently take flight into day-dreaming; far away from where you are located in time and place as well as in discursive and emotional content. Anyone working at a task requiring immense concentration, such as performing brain surgery or washing the windows of a high-rise building in the wind, is well served by dissociating from ordinary day-to-day personal concerns. All these may be considered as within the normal

---

[10]The initial criterion for diagnosing DID is: A. Disruption of identity characterized by two or more distinct personality states. This involves marked discontinuity in sense of self and sense of agency, accompanied by related alterations in affect, behavior, consciousness, memory, perception, cognition, and sensory-motor functioning. DSM-5 (300.14).

range of dissociation found in ordinary people.

The range of dissociation stretches from these common examples to dissociative disorders such as the psychogenic amnesia associated with traumatized victims. In these disorders, there is a periodic detachment from self, where one feels unreal, or from one's surroundings, where one feels the outside world is unreal. At the extreme end of the spectrum one finds DID.

DID is characterized by the presence of two or more personality states that behave independently, as if they are separate people. These personality states, referred to as alters, have different reactions, emotions, autobiographical memories, and sometimes even different physiological functioning. For example, there may be a 30 year old timid and shy woman acting as a host personality, with a tough street-fighter "protector" second identity, and a coquettish and seductive third identity. Hiding behind these would likely be a few child-alters who are still holding unresolved memories of past trauma.

For DID patients, pathological dissociation originates under the assault of trauma. Within the fragmentation of ego that results, the separate personality states arise and appear to serve specific functions, based on certain internal and external needs. People with DID have serious memory gaps, referred to as "time-loss." They often have no knowledge of what was said or done by alters who had assumed control of the body.

The link between early childhood trauma and the fragmentation of personal identity is often hidden. Because the alters do not self-identify as alternate personalities, the phenomenon of DID is often missed. When they do reveal themselves by appearing split-off from the host, their appearance may be misconstrued as manifestations of a histrionic personality. To the observer who is not empathic or aware of the background from which alters emerge, the appearance of alters may be seen as a sign of psychosis.

Through my experience with Joan, one can see how the appearance of an alter could only be understood in the context of past history of early childhood abuse. Had SW appeared without calling me stupid and pointing out his own gender, it would not have been so easy to identify him as an alter. I might have missed it, presuming that Joan was simply angry about something I didn't catch.

Dramatic personality switches between alternate personalities provide rich fodder for creative writers and actors.[11] These portrayals have been written primarily as entertainment, however, not as accurate clinical portraits of highly distressed human beings in pain. Clinical findings of ongoing physical, sexual and incestuous abuse in someone's early childhood is not entertaining, but that is generally the etiology of DID.

Some therapists believe that DID is akin to a "Jekyll and Hyde" syndrome. Robert Louis Stevenson's novelette *The Strange Case of Dr. Jekyll and Mr. Hyde,* is well-known, having been first published in 1886 and later adapted into more than a hundred movies. It is an allegorical tale of good and evil. It is about the dark side of human beings, and temptations to act it out. It is not about DID.

Dissociation is an adaptive response to trauma. With long standing early recurrent trauma, DID occurs spontaneously as a response to extreme and critical

---

[11] As recently as 2009-2011, a popular TV comedy-drama based on that theme, entitled the United States of Tara, earned numerous nominations and awards.

psychological needs. When a person encounters repeated distress triggering the same emotions, situations, or physiological arousal as old traumas, dissociation and splitting will likely occur as that adaptive response becomes habituated.

The alters, along with the host personality, should be considered a system. While it is certainly possible that there are those alters within the system that direct violence toward other people the system may encounter, this has not been the case with the alters that I have seen in my practice. The alters which the internal system characterize as evil are primarily self-destructive, not inclined to seek the destruction of other people.

Books and movies such as *The Three Faces of Eve*, popular in the 1950s, or *Sybil*, popular in the 1970s, have been the bases from which the general public derives its incomplete and inaccurate information concerning MPD.

Sybil[12] is the story of a young woman suffering from MPD who was treated by Dr. Cornelia B. Wilbur in the 1950s and 1960s. The author, Flora Rheta Schreiber, personally knew both Sybil, a pseudonym for the patient, and Dr. Wilbur. She claimed to have reviewed every single document connected with Sybil's eleven years of psychoanalysis. These included Dr. Wilbur's daily notes taken over the course of Sybil's 2,354 sessions of psychoanalysis, Sybil's essays written as part of the treatment procedure, and tape recordings of some of the analytic sessions. One must keep in mind that Schreiber, without psychoanalytic training, was trying to understand what Dr. Wilbur was actually doing during therapy while simultaneously creating a mass-marketable literary property.

---

[12] *Sybil* by Flora Rheta Schreiber. Grand Central Publishing. 2009.

The book has been blamed for creating a social milieu that turned the phenomenon of MPD into a fad. It was so popular that I actually had a patient ask me, "Do I have MPD, like Sybil?" Accepting for the moment that Sybil was an early example of an MPD sufferer, it is instructive to compare her diagnosis and treatment to what we know about DID today.

The first few pages of the book describe Sybil's bewilderment after finding herself in the disorientation of time-loss. This is one of the cardinal and classical presentations of DID. In fact, many of my patients were prompted to seek therapy after similarly finding themselves in a strange place, disoriented after hours or days of time-loss.

Sybil's traumatic history is typical of DID patients. Sybil's psychotic mother subjected her to years of physical and emotional abuse from which she had no escape. She hated looking at herself in the mirror, vehemently resisted acknowledging the alters, and refused to listen to their recorded voices. The resistance to know about alters is also characteristic of DID patients I have seen. These experiences and behaviors, so similar to those expressed by my DID patients, convinces me that Sybil was suffering from DID. At the time Sybil was written, neither DID nor these experiences so common to DID patients, were known to the general public or even to the general psychiatric community.

Dr. Wilbur followed the practice of Freudian psychoanalysis and immediately focused on sexual issues. The book focuses on Sybil's witnessing her parents having sexual intercourse as if it were a highly significant trauma in Sybil's early life. A contemporary therapist would likely ignore this primal scene. In many places throughout the world, the whole family lives in one room, and often several families live under one roof. Seeing human sexuality is something that must be common where many people live in such crowded conditions.

Dr. Wilbur conducted psychoanalysis on Sybil's main personality and the system's 15 alters. This lengthy treatment is neither practical nor likely necessary. The most difficult patient that I have treated, Ruth (Chapter 5), was involuntarily kept in the hospital continuously for five months prior to seeing me. She was successfully treated with less than 500 therapeutic hours distributed over the course of two and a half years. Ruth is an example of rapid progress in treatment and is not a predictor of the time frame required for other patients' therapy. I have never had a DID patient whose course of treatment required anywhere near the number of sessions Dr. Wilbur conducted with Sybil.

Today, trauma should be at the forefront of the therapist's index of suspicion in such a case. Without understanding that the core issue of DID is trauma, too much attention may be given to multiplicity. It is critical to remember that alters are not entertainment.

I never got to know the alters of my patients very well, seeing them only as necessary when they presented problems in the day-to-day functioning of the whole system. Multiplicity is the manifestation of dissociation, the product of trauma. The trauma needs to be the focus, and it needs to be healed.

Therapeutic boundaries are more clearly defined today than in Dr. Wilbur's time. Psychiatrists advisedly do not mix professional relationship and friendship with their patients. However, Dr. Wilbur had a very close relationship with Sybil outside the office. It may be that she thought her surrogate motherhood might provide a corrective emotional experience for the patient to mature and develop in a safe place as well as to process the traumatic memory.

Considering that the diagnosis of MPD was hardly recognized at that time, and that there were no known treatment guidelines, Dr. Wilbur had nothing to go by but the standard psychoanalytic practices of the day. In that light, one should view Dr. Wilbur as a pioneer in MPD treatment.

Sybil eventually recanted her multiplicity. In the eyes of many, this did much to discredit the legitimacy of MPD as a diagnosis. It was suggested that she was a hysteric whose doctor implanted the ideas of these personalities, and that in a moment of clarity she denied the multiplicity as nonsense.[13]

In my experience, such denial is not an uncommon phenomenon. It does not necessarily mean that the diagnosis is incorrect. It's relevant to note that Sybil later wrote letters re-affirming her belief in the existence of her multiplicity both to her doctor and to a friend. The nature of the inner family of MPD is such that there are bound to be differing opinions expressed at different times by alters who may or may not have access to each other.

---

[13] *Sybil Exposed*, written by Debbie Nathan (Free Press, 2012), evaluated the events presented in *Sybil*. Nathan claims that the allegedly true story outlined in the book was largely fabricated. Without entering that debate, the book Sybil raised awareness of MPD into the public consciousness. Proving it to be a work of fiction in no way impacts the validity of a clinical diagnosis of MPD. To wit, the composer Freiderich Chopin has always been assumed to have died from pulmonary tuberculosis, but recent theories suggest that his death might be from cystic fibrosis. If this were indeed proven true, it would not invalidate the diagnostic category of the disease of pulmonary tuberculosis.

The sensationalism around the story of Sybil is a far cry from the reality of day-to-day treatment of patients with MPD who are suffering from the trauma of decades' past. The nature and depth of the disorder dwarfs any dramatic fictional entertainment in books, TV, or movies.

Therapists familiar with DID will recognize Sybil's conduct as concordant with DID. Even if her childhood trauma could not be proven in a court of law, it does not invalidate the diagnosis. People who argue against the diagnostic classification of DID keep missing this important point.

Chapter 3 Sandra - Recognizing DID

Not all my patients presented as dramatically as Joan. Neither did all respond so remarkably to therapy. I did meet with failure. In the beginning, I failed to even detect clearly presenting DID or to find a way to treat this complex disorder.

I met Sandra in the early 1970s, a decade after beginning my psychiatric practice. She was the first patient I encountered with MPD. The fact that I missed the diagnosis, which in retrospect appears so obvious, had a great influence on me. It stimulated my interest in Multiple Personality Disorder, as DID was then called.

Sandra was a single woman in her twenties, depressed and in distress. Having graduated from university, she seemed to have lost her direction in life. Living on her own, she was estranged from family and friends. From time to time, when she needed the money, Sandra would deliver pamphlets or telephone directories door to door.

She seemed to be held back by something in her private inner world. After struggling for the right word, she finally found "nadir" to express her sense of despair. She was otherwise unable to say more. I understood that she was in pain, but I could not get a feel for what she was going through.

Together, we examined both the present and the past, but nothing seemed to shift for her. My later years of experience would have helped me to wade through her several smoke screens and quickly get to the crux of the matter. At the time, however, I could not find any opening to apply Cognitive Therapy. Medications that alleviated depression in others did not help her.

Sandra then told me that she had some momentary "lapses." She described them as experiences where she was "out," then "came to." She felt as if she was possessed by another being and, in that state, had done things that she would not normally have done. I was totally unprepared for such a confession. I did not even think of asking her to elaborate. The scenario was so foreign to me that I didn't know how to respond. Tentatively, she asked if she could be suffering from MPD.

At the time, I barely recognized the term. MPD was something assumed to be so rare that it had not even been mentioned in my extensive psychiatric training. Rather than seeing her time and memory lapses as a possible tip-off for MPD, I wondered whether she might be suffering from some temporal lobe dysfunction. Stuck in my role as a neuro-psychiatrist scanning for physical explanations, I missed seeing what Sandra had placed squarely before me. Armed with what I know today, a few more questions in the right direction would have clarified matters and almost clinched the diagnosis of MPD.

Sandra did not come back to see me. At the time, I did not know why. Now, I can imagine how let down she must have felt.

A few years later, I happened to sit next to Sandra's last doctor at a social event. The doctor told me that she thought Sandra was suffering from MPD. We compared notes and, based on experience I had since gained, I agreed. Unfortunately, even having the correctly identified diagnosis did not reverse the course of her pathology. Treatment was unsuccessful: Sandra committed suicide. I cannot say for sure that the ultimate result would have been different if, at the time I saw her, I had possessed the knowledge and skill I later developed. I think it would have given Sandra at least a fighting chance at healing.

In those days, MPD was an even more unfamiliar diagnosis than today. In the unlikely event of a correct diagnosis, treatment by specialists was more focused on exploring the original trauma than healing the wound. Treatment options were generally unknown or untested. They often involved employing drastic measures such as intravenous Sodium Amytal[14] interviews. I would caution against such interviews. Those measures may permit traumatic memories to surface, but without the tools to enable their processing, it will prove counterproductive. It is far safer, and actually quicker in the overall scheme of therapy, to allow the system to determine the engagement with alters and traumatic memories.

Therapeutic Keys

A patient who mentions experiences of time-loss must raise one's index of suspicion concerning DID. Sandra's expressions of being "out" and "coming back" coupled with doing things that she would not have ordinarily done – indicated by purchases of items the host would never have bought or finding oneself in a place the

---

[14]Sodium amylo-barbitone is a barbiturate used intravenously to relax a patient so as to facilitate their talking; in these cases, about the original trauma. In early days of MPD treatment, therapists were more concerned about finding out the original trauma than helping the patient handle its effects in their current life. Today, the emphasis has moved to focusing on how the trauma is impacting the patient's current functioning.

host would never have gone, are extremely important warning signs.

Proper diagnosis is paramount, but without applying proper therapeutic methods to process the underlying trauma, one cannot effectively help the patient.

Chapter 4 Leila - A House Divided

My second MPD patient, the first one that I recognized as such, was Leila. Leila began therapy with me in the late 1970s and continued for a turbulent 13 years. It was through interacting with Leila and her alters that I understood that MPD is undeniable. Although I did my best to help her, I had not yet developed any framework for treating this complex disorder. I was ultimately unable to provide effective therapeutic intervention.

The host was timid and self-effacing. She was extremely kind and considerate of others. She never blamed anyone for her difficulties, not even her abuser. I met several of Leila's alters, but two personalities stood out as very distinct. There was a terrified child alter who was living totally in fear of the past and a second alter who was a confident, charming and coquettish adult. All of the alters appeared in the context of our psychotherapy sessions. During this period of time, the patient was severely anorexic and suicidal.

Leila was a frail child-like housewife in her early forties, living with her kind and compassionate husband. They were childless after 8 years of marriage. According to the referral letter from her family doctor, her chief complaints were chronic depression and a strong aversion to sex. In addition, she was taking what appeared to be too many prescription sleeping pills. After engaging in therapy with two psychiatrists and one psychologist, she was referred to me.

Leila was one of the most anxious and fearful people I had ever met. She sat hunched in a chair across from me, legs intertwined like the stems of a vine. She complained of tightness in her chest and difficulty in breathing. I asked Leila to close her eyes and just slow down her breathing. Instead, it became more labored as her body stiffened even further. When I asked her gently why she was so tense, she smiled sadly and denied any tension.

Her increased anxiety, when asked to simply pay attention to her breathing, would now alert me to the possibility of some deep psychopathology. I recognized her as someone gravely traumatized. She appeared to be half-aware of some tight knot or deep pain inside, and was afraid to get close to it. Leila's extreme tension persisted throughout her sessions with me. When I asked her why she seemed unhappy and why she was losing weight, she evaded the issues by quickly answering, "No, I am not." This response was always accompanied by a painful smile.

Although she quickly grew attached to me, we were making no progress with her psychotherapy. She denied having had any unusual or adverse childhood experiences. At the same time, she claimed to have no childhood memories before the age of 15. I became convinced that she had been traumatized in childhood. We seemed at an impasse.

Some months into the therapy, her husband told me that he found Leila huddled in a corner of their bed one night. She was whimpering, sobbing, and mumbling like a three year old child. She was shaking in fear. It had taken him a long time to calm her down. He asked me outright if she could have "what they call a multiple personality disorder." He also told me how he could "bring out that child part," by gently stroking her hair.

As noted, I was struggling to find a way to treat the trauma. So, with great reluctance, I touched her hair. I would now invite such a spouse into the session before doing something like this as such conduct is pushing the boundaries of psychiatric propriety. I absolutely do not recommend this as an example to follow, yet, at the time, I saw no other option. I felt it was necessary to gently explore this so as to be able to confirm or deny the MPD suggested by her husband. Suddenly, out came a small frightened child. She was looking at me with teary eyes and begging me not to hurt her. She kept calling me "Grandpa."

The transformation from woman to small frightened child was instantaneous. It was accompanied by a startled expression and a reflexive recoiling away from me. Fear clearly registered in her whole demeanor. This evidence of absolute dissociation, including her inability to recognize me as her doctor, forced me to make the diagnosis of MPD. Not believing in possession by evil spirits, I had no other explanation for this phenomenon.

No matter what I said or did, she was unable to recognize me as her doctor, or even that we were in a doctor's office. The scene lasted several minutes. It terminated with her "waking up" as a much dazed and distressed Leila, with no memory of the frightened little girl.

One evening not long after this event, a police officer called me. The police had responded to a call for help from a woman who had taken an overdose. He asked me to speak to the fire-captain of the emergency response team. The team had gone to Leila's house and were forced to break a window to gain access.

The fire-captain told me that he first encountered a woman in her forties who appeared extremely frightened, shaking like a leaf. Then, in a matter of seconds, she suddenly "switched" into a mature, poised, and collected lady, "like a totally different person." She calmly thanked him, and informed him that she was "feeling fine." She had just taken a couple of extra sleeping pills, but she would be all right. "Could this be a (case of) multiple personality?" he asked.

It had taken him seconds to come to the correct diagnosis. The experience of multiple alters appearing within moments of each other in a stress laden situation must have been undeniable. This kind of clear direct experience does not generally happen in a consultation room. As a fully qualified specialist in psychiatry with many years of experience at that time, and having practiced on three continents, it had taken me many months to come to that same conclusion. In fact, I came to that conclusion only after Leila's husband provided the key. It is likely that some psychiatrists have never recognized a case of MPD because they have never directly engaged with multiple alters in a stress scenario as did the fire-captain, or that no one presented them with the key as Leila's husband did for me.

When an MPD patient experiences a crisis, alters come out. They may deal with it individually, or they make take turns assuming control and influencing the unfolding of events. It is likely that several alters exerted control over the host, Leila, at different times that night.

Leila's husband was out of town on a consulting job that particular night, and a depressed alter made an ambivalent attempt to take an over-dose, but not enough to kill herself. When she went to bed, a more protective alter took charge and placed the emergency call to 911 for help. When the rescue team arrived, it was the probably the anxiety ridden host personality that faced the emergency response team as they entered. Finally, another alter took charge, telling the fire-captain, "Everything is fine, thank you very much."

Leila's Early Trauma

I had not yet developed the skill to approach the alters to help Leila process the trauma.

Like Joan's husband Ken, Leila's husband gathered much information about her past trauma through his many night-time conversations with some of her alters. Her childhood babysitter every Saturday for many years was her paternal grandfather. A very warped and sadistic man, he abused and tortured her. Absorbed in her own life, Leila's mother was completely unaware of her daughter's plight.

A question naturally arises, "How could her mother have missed Leila's distress before and after every babysitting by the grandfather?" I would not be surprised if the mother also had experienced abuse. Parents who had been abused as children tend to have a blind spot concerning the warning signs of abuse happening to their own children. As a result, and perhaps because of the failure to deal with their own abuse, they are unable to protect their children. When I wanted to speak with Leila's mother to gain some background information, Leila absolutely refused. She was very protective of her mother, who was suffering from poor health at the time. Leila never blamed anyone but herself for her grandfather's conduct.

As time went on, Leila's file became thick with letters. These letters came to me from her husband as well as from different alters. Unfortunately, I did not know how to proceed with her therapy. At that time, in the late 1970s, the first textbook on diagnosis and treatment of MPD had yet to be published. In standard general psychiatric textbooks, MPD was considered more of a curiosity than a disorder psychiatrists might actually encounter. Information about MPD was, at most, contained on one page. Some textbooks failed to even mention MPD.

Always polite and compliant in therapy, Leila seemed comforted and satisfied in seeing me once a week. However, therapy was not progressing. Like Sybil, Leila refused to accept that there were alters coming out to speak directly to me and to her husband. Leila's husband supplied me with the information he gained at night from the alters, which I tried to use in the therapy.

Whenever the fearful alter came out in my office, Leila's body shook in terror. She pleaded with me not to hurt her, always confusing me with her abuser. Nothing I did or said could change that.

Her husband told me about another trigger he had discovered. Whispering the words "my little princess" would cause Leila to have a major flashback: The fearful alter appeared immediately. Afterwards, the host personality would return in a daze. The host never accepted my report that another identity had appeared in my office. The personality switches were neither theatrical nor entertaining. They were extremely painful to witness.

I repeatedly brought out the fearful child part, hoping to provide a corrective emotional experience by reassuring her that she was safe. I believed that if the fearful alters had come out and were able to be comforted, it would have resulted in therapeutic gains. Unfortunately, as attached to me as she seemed, we were unable to establish a sufficient therapeutic alliance from within which she could work on her past trauma. The frightened child alter could never see me as her doctor.

Recall of traumatic implicit memory causes a powerful upheaval in the autonomic nervous system. Leila's speechless terror was easily triggered into manifesting externally. However, even when not manifesting, it remained a permanent fixture locked in her body.[15] This alter was stuck in an apparently endless replay of intrusive thoughts and images of the horrific abuse.

I was unable to comfort the severely traumatized fragmented part. From the vantage point of my later years of experience, after failing to comfort the child the first time, I would have refrained from trying to bring her out. I would have sought to establish a stronger therapeutic alliance, perhaps through different alters, to make her feel secure enough to present in her own time.

It would have been helpful to have had a mentor with experience, one who could have given me helpful feedback and perhaps pointed out potential next steps to me. Even if I had read Sybil at the time, following Dr. Wilbur's treatment would not have been helpful. In my

---

[15]Some examples of explicit memory include recalling a movie or a telephone number. Implicit memory pertains to remembering how to ride a bicycle, which it is not something you can easily use words to describe. In a simplified scheme, the amygdala (a part of the mid brain) determines the emotional significance of any given data, influencing the hippocampus (another part of the mid-brain) how to store the memory data. Excessive stimulation of the amygdala interferes with hippocampal functioning, inhibiting cognitive evaluation of experience and semantic representation. A terrorized child therefore stores the information as implicit memory, in a non-verbal way, so that on recall, all the child experiences are somatic sensations and visual images. This is what is characterized aptly as: "Speechless terror."

experience, intravenous barbiturate and ECT are not beneficial in the treatment for MPD.

Psychotherapy for MPD patients involves treading on deep pain and suffering from the past. There are grave risks of re-traumatization involving life and death matters. From very early on, it was clear to me that re-traumatization is the most important thing to avoid in MPD therapy. I knew that calling out a terrified alter without being able to provide a corrective emotional experience was tantamount to re-traumatizing her. This would further ingrain the pre-existing damage rather than generating a gateway to healing from it.

It is possible that there was another alter guarding Leila to ensure that she would never trust a person in a position of power that could harm her. The tight amnestic barriers were able to protect the rest of the system from remembering the trauma, but not from the ravages that the traumatic experience had inflicted on the whole system.

Leila's body continued to be bound by tension, and I, too, was stalled. I was unable to see a therapeutic path forward. During one session in which I brought out the frightened girl begging not to be hurt, I stopped talking and just waited. The whimpering child suddenly stopped crying. She sat up, and transformed herself into a sophisticated lady with a charming smile. I remember the sense of shock, and the shiver that ran up my spine.

What I encountered was a confident, poised and even a little coquettish adult. She spoke with a distinctive Southern accent. The terrified child disappeared. The inhibited, fearful, and self-effacing Leila was now this Southern belle, speaking to me as an equal. She was charming, delighting in teasing me. I found myself a little tongue-tied. My capacity to switch therapeutic reference points could not catch up with the rapidity of her personality switch. Again from the vantage point of my later accumulated experience, it is clear that one must be prepared for such rapid changes.

I understand now that this alter, and others, were created to enable Leila to cope with the terror that arose during flashbacks of the past abuse. Switching into this light-hearted Texas belle, full of humor, charm and having an entirely philosophical outlook in life, gave Leila some temporary relief.

Eventually, I learned that there were at least ten alters. From time to time, two of them would write to me. I accepted the information they delivered but regret that I was not flexible enough to exploit these opportunities and respond to them directly. Based on my lack of training and experience in MPD, I was exclusively focused on working with the host and the one terrified alter who only saw me as her "grandpa."

Leila, the host, was severely depressed while taking more and more tranquilizers for her tension. I resorted to doling out her pills weekly so that she would not have too many pills on hand at once. Although pharmaceutical intervention was the accepted protocol for depression, the medications provided no relief. She continued to lose weight slowly and steadily. Finally, she had to be admitted to the hospital so her doctors could investigate the weight loss. Nothing came of those investigations.

The host was always the submissive and self-effacing Leila. The block to her recovery, and the ultimate danger she faced, was that she was incapable of getting in touch with the energy of anger that might have effected change. It was likely that there were angry alters remaining hidden within the inner world. When Leila was finally able to speak about her abuser, she insisted that all the abuse heaped upon her was justified. Years of therapy could not change her stated belief that, "I was a bad little girl and I deserved it."

One day, within this turmoil, a promiscuous alter surfaced. This alter spoke of meeting someone in a seedy downtown hotel. The innocent and inhibited Leila was absolutely ignorant of this. I had no way of knowing if it was a fantasy, a threat, or an actual extra-marital affair. I had become an impotent therapist hoping that what I was hearing was not true.

As I focused all my attention on the timid host and the terrified alter-ego, perhaps even a casual observer today can suggest what I might have done differently. I had been presented with a willing and motivated patient. Some alters were eager to communicate. Leila had a caring and supportive husband. Totally focused on the terrified alter, I had failed to seize what would now appear as obvious opportunities to access Leila's inner world. The therapeutic path was potentially wide open but I was unable to step outside of the standard therapeutic approach.

Therapeutic Impasse

I went through excruciating self-doubt with Leila. She presented tremendous instability, sometimes threatening suicide and repeatedly speaking of terminating therapy. For two years, she would phone my office an hour before every one of her appointments to inform me that she would not be coming. My secretary always alerted me, and

I always called Leila back. She would be waiting by the phone. On hearing my voice, she invariably changed her mind and came to my office. I never said anything more than simply, "Leila, are you sure you want to cancel?"

It was a contest of perseverance. It is likely that there was one alter who wanted to quit and made the calls to cancel the appointments. But when I called back, another alter, on behalf of herself and others who wanted to continue seeing me, got a boost of resolve. That alter would then take over, and Leila would come to see me.

I was unsure if I had the right to influence her wish to end therapy. She certainly had the right to do so, but I worried that the phone calls I made, resulting in her changing her mind every time, were unprofessional. I asked myself if she was playing a game and, if so, what might be her ulterior motive. I considered whether I simply needed to respect that part of her wishing to quit, and leave her in peace.

In these calls, however, I was careful not to pressure her to come back. I limited each call to merely confirm if it was her wish to quit coming to see me. I now know that such vacillation is not uncommon and quite understandable in the context of DID psychopathology.

I discussed these concerns with her husband, who was reasonable, understanding and sympathetic. He was quite clear that Leila would refuse any referral to another psychiatrist, even simply to get a second opinion. Besides, there was no one else in the community willing or able to take her on as a patient. Leila's husband also predicted, in a matter of fact way, that she would eventually kill herself if and when she stopped seeing me. Without colleagues to call upon for guidance and help, I started to question my own motives in continuing with her.

One day, I told her I would let her go and wished her luck. She was visibly relieved and thanked me, with tears in her eyes. Her husband fully accepted the decision.

Eighteen months after she stopped therapy, Leila's husband informed me that she passed away following an overdose of sleeping pills. Calmly, he thanked me for "keeping her alive and comforting her for 13 years." Even though I had been expecting that call, the news left me speechless and deeply sad. I believe that she waited those 18 months out of concern for my feelings.

A total of 500 therapeutic hours were spent on Leila. Despite my training and experience, without effective therapeutic guidelines to follow, the correct diagnosis alone was not sufficient to effectively help her. Although I had done my best for 13 years, even the acknowledgment of her husband did not erase my sadness.

At the time, it did not occur to me that there had been another option. If I had approached the willing alters and engaged them in a dialogue, I might have gained access through them that would have proven useful leverage in therapy. The best therapeutic strategy would have been to make that first step to gain access to her inner world of multiplicity.

I had yet to learn a key principle of MPD treatment; to treat each single MPD patient as if I was conducting group therapy. Knowing they are all listening, one can start talking to them as a group. Leila paid a huge price for me to learn this key principle.

I feel compelled now to pass on what Leila, Sandra, and my other DID patients have taught me, so that the collective experience I gained from them can be utilized by other therapists and mental health workers in recognizing and treating DID patients.

Therapeutic Keys

For MPD "group" therapy, the group consists of the host and the alters. Despite a patient's fierce denial of the presence of alters, if they have appeared in therapy, the therapist should understand that whatever the therapist says is being heard by all of the alters. When working with one alter, one must always include an acknowledgment of the others. A simple acknowledgment of this internal world can have tremendous positive impact.

When an alter is willing to communicate directly, either verbally or through letters, the therapist should always acknowledge them. Through that acknowledgment, one can gain access to the inner DID world. With such access, crucial additional support can often be found inside.

Engaging Multiple Personalities – Volume 1

Chapter 5   Ruth – Trapped in Misdiagnoses

Ruth was diagnosed with, and treated for, chronic depression most of her life. In the year prior to seeing me, she had been held in the hospital psychiatric ward for five continuous months because of repeated suicide attempts. Despite consulting with numerous doctors, including specialists, no one had ever considered that she might be suffering from trauma, much less the possibility of DID. This case illustrates a most important point: Treatment based on an incorrect diagnosis is doomed to failure.

By the age of 28, Ruth already had 20 hospital admissions for depression. She was married to an abusive man with whom she'd had two sons, but was no longer living with him. Because of her recurrent hospitalizations and mental health difficulties, her immediate family sent the boys, ages 1½ and 3 years old, to relatives in USA. Believing that she was not capable of parenting, they wanted the relatives to adopt the children. Ruth had come to see me in the hope that she could become well enough to recover her children.

In the subdued light of my waiting room, Ruth held herself very still. A young, shy, slightly plump woman, she wore a modest head covering and a long pale blue dress stamped with a faint floral pattern. Although she had a studied calm that day, I learned later that the billowing sleeves of her blouse covered self-inflicted scars that traveled down her upper arms to her wrists.

Ruth was no stranger to the doctors and staff of the emergency department in her hometown hospital. During the five month involuntary hospitalization, her diagnosis was psychotic depression.

Knowing that she had driven nine hours to see me, I had reserved two hours on two consecutive days to see her. As soon as she came into my office, she began recounting her history chronologically in a clear voice. She knew exactly what she needed to tell me, and I listened without interruption.

Epilepsy

Ruth had suffered from epilepsy since childhood. She was raised in a tightly knit rural religious community in the prairies, the seventh of eight children. Her mother, over-burdened with so many children, seemed resentful of having to care for a sick child. Ruth could remember only punishment and angry outbursts from her mother. She described her father as having been kind to her, but seldom around because of work. I sensed that it was more a wishful thinking than a fact.[16] From the age of three, she felt abandoned and worthless.

Ruth's epileptic seizures made her feel like the odd one out. Her mother sought to treat the seizures with a very strict diet that further identified her as "different" than others. The seizures often resulted in her being humiliated by her own family.

As she retreated inward, the only living creatures she could relate to were the dairy cows on the family farm. At 20, she had a brain operation for uncontrollable seizures.

---

[16]Ruth's father's lack of empathy and concern with his daughter's alienation and isolation, and his lack of support to her needs may be construed as a form of abuse. This case reminds me of Sybil's father, who denied his responsibility to be a protecting parent when stating, "It is a mother's place to raise the child."

This operation was successful in controlling her epilepsy, but she remained on a regimen of anticonvulsant medications. Soon after this operation, she was given a course of ECT on the recommendation of the Mood Disorder Clinic for her depression. ECT is, effectively, a medically induced epileptic seizure that has been shown to help with depression in many patients. For Ruth, spontaneously occurring epileptic seizures had not cured her depression in 20 years, nor did this course of ECT.

I believe that she was treated only by "biological psychiatrists" who base their practice almost exclusively on using medication for treatment and patient management. This approach tends to consider DID as being non-existent, and if it is acknowledged, it is considered iatrogenic, (meaning that it is caused by other therapists in treatment). They have no way to conceptualize dissociation in ego-fragmentation other than to see it as the expression of an attention-seeking hysteric[17]. They did not explore with Ruth the impact of trauma and possibility of dissociation.

Church and Faith

Although Ruth was a devoted church member, she remained different; always depressed and a loner. Church members considered her depression and her epilepsy demonic. They accused her of seeking attention and, worse

---

[17]My view is that the term "attention-seeking" should be abolished from psychiatric writing. It is a term that has deteriorated into one of dismissal. Anyone who is suffering and seeking therapy has a right to receive attention from their helping professional. Because of repeated suicide attempts, Ruth was treated as a "hysteric," another pejorative term no longer of value in psychiatry. The ongoing dismissals of Ruth's complaints were likely facilitated through the abidance of such pejorative terms.

still, of being possessed. Their fervent prayers for the devil to leave her did nothing to help Ruth fit into her family, school, or community.

The more alienated she became, the more other church members criticized her in front of the whole congregation. They viewed her alienation as a lack of faith. They repeatedly exhorted her to confess her sins.

Like many abused women, Ruth came to expect harsh, sadistic treatment. This was indeed what she received from her husband when she married at the age of 24. After one particularly nasty incident, the police placed her and the children in a safe house.

While the separation from her husband had given Ruth a reprieve from her great distress, her church frowned upon divorce. The head of the church exerted considerable pressure on Ruth to reconcile with her husband.

Symptom and Treatment History

Soon after her epilepsy surgery, she had received a series of ten ECTs for depression. These treatments were unsuccessful. Since then, she had cycled through severe depressions, self-mutilations, and many hospital admissions.

Her psychiatric treatment had always been based on medications. By the time Ruth met with me, she was on hefty dosages of antipsychotic, antidepressant and anticonvulsant drugs. While anticonvulsant medications are often given to epileptics, they are also used for psychiatric purposes as they can have a mood-stabilizing effect as well as an augmenting effect on antidepressants.

She had ongoing bouts of time-loss that lasted from many hours to days. She had no idea what she did or where she went during these episodes. She could hear voices within her mind arguing. They gave her instructions to cut herself, to be a proper mother, or to go be with "Satan."[18] Ruth engaged in dialogues with the voices as if they were discrete individuals.

She remembered that these voices had started in childhood. She then traced back the fragmentation of her mind. The first split had occurred at age three following a harsh punishment from her mother. Ruth initially brought out a list of 17 parts, which she called person A, person B, person C and so on. She had rudimentary descriptions of each. She could hear these voices chattering away.

For so long as she could remember, Ruth had practiced self-mutilation daily both to punish herself and to draw blood that she could give to Satan. Once, she deliberately pushed a sewing needle into the muscle of her left upper arm. The doctors decided that surgical removal would have caused massive damage to the muscles and severe blood loss. The needle remains in her arm even today.

Until quite recently, Ruth had no memory of her life between the ages of 12 and 24.

---

[18]This reference may be to the Biblical fallen angel or to the abuser specifically. I did not seek to define which it was. It is possible that the reference was to the specific abuser representing the qualities of Satan. It is just as likely that it was a reference to the metaphorical battle she felt internally – being pulled in one direction by Satan and in the other direction by God. It could be a conflation of the two. The exact referent was not relevant to therapy.

Ruth's Secrets

Ruth carried a dark secret. It is possible that her family did not know the secret. It is also possible that they did but brushed it aside, choosing to ignore it. The secret was that Ruth had been serially raped and molested. She was first raped at the age of seven by two neighbors, a father and son. Those neighbors continued to sexually abuse Ruth. More molestations followed, perpetrated by, in Ruth's words, other neighborhood bullies. Some of these perpetrators were known to the community and to the police, but they had never been tried nor brought to justice.

For many years, Ruth kept that secret to herself. She never told the teachers or doctors who counseled her in connection with her depression. Ruth had no memory of her further abuse until she was questioned by the police as part of an investigation of one of her later principal abusers. They were trying to gather evidence to bring charges against that person. This was three years before she came to see me.

During the police questioning, some additional memories returned. She told her abuse history to a police officer and a counselor. At 17, while Ruth's parents were 500 miles away, her sister-in-law took Ruth to that in-law's own father. This man was the object of the police investigation. Ruth described him as Satanic. He lived in an isolated area with guns and dogs. He was highly skilled in mind-control. Terrorizing her at gun point, he used hypnosis to bond her to him and to see him as her lover. She returned to him repeatedly to be abused. This continued about three times a week for months, then sporadically for years.

These returned memories were accompanied and

followed by panic-filled flashbacks. There was an increased intensity of the self-mutilations.

Ruth warned me not to use certain words as they would trigger panic and flashbacks. Relax, dogs, beard, mustache, dark room, therapist, bathing and nudity were the triggers. Merely suggesting that she be photographed would generate a flashback.

Diagnosis

After listening to Ruth's history, I had no difficulty making a provisional diagnosis of DID. This was all that was needed to proceed with therapy. There was no urgency to confirm the diagnosis. Indeed, having an urgency to do so can be counterproductive. The diagnosis was confirmed in its own time by direct interaction with Ruth's alters.

Ruth was not interested in the diagnostic label of DID. She was resentful of being given yet another diagnostic label. However, her determination to get better so that she could recover her children was far more important to her.

It was obvious that Ruth had been severely traumatized. Verbal cues reminded her of terrifying past experiences, triggering her into dissociation. The voices arguing within her head were a crowd of dissociated alters produced during the abuses.

When encountering patients complaining of hearing voices, the classical index of suspicion suggests the possibility of schizophrenia. However, schizophrenia is primarily a thinking disorder. Ruth was so logical and organized in her speech that I easily ruled out such a diagnosis.

Ruth had felt constant rejection from her family, community and church. She emphasized that throughout her life she had been criticized and judged. None of her suffering had ever been acknowledged.

She had been married to an abusive husband, from whom she obtained a separation only after a very hard-fought battle. The church minister had opposed her choice to leave her violent husband. The church scapegoated her as a faithless sinner. Her children had been taken to another country without her consent. Her depression had not responded to ECT or any pharmaceutical anti-depressant. Her future did not look promising. Considering her history and circumstances, the depression she exhibited should be seen as an appropriate emotional response rather than a pathology.

The story of sexual abuse by a "Satanic" abuser seemed bizarre. With Ruth's permission, I contacted the police officer who had been in charge of investigating this person. In a long phone conversation, he confirmed that one of Ruth's abusers was well known to the police. This abuser had masqueraded as a therapist to net his victims. He had indeed used guns and dogs as part of his abusive pattern.

There were other victims besides Ruth, but the police were unable to gather enough evidence to bring charges. The officer had interrogated Ruth for hours as they tried to compile evidence. The police concluded that the haziness of Ruth's memories would make her a poor witness in court. Their questioning of her left unintended consequences that included Ruth's flashbacks, escalating self-mutilations, and hospital admissions.

Also with Ruth's permission, I phoned and spoke to one of her former schoolteachers. This individual had known Ruth since high school. She verbally confirmed Ruth's story, then sent me two ten-page letters written in longhand giving a detailed account of her early life. These confirmed the veracity of Ruth's traumatic experiences with her family and community.

Effects of Trauma: From Childhood through Adolescence and into Adulthood

As a young child, Ruth underwent prolonged sexual and emotional abuse. Later, she was the target of sexual, emotional, and physical abuse. The emotional abuse came from the cold rejection by people in her family, especially her mother, and her conservative rural community.

Ruth had been shamed by the epileptic seizures that were sometimes accompanied by loss of bladder and/or bowel control. She became a marked victim for sexual abuse in her community. Once a victim, she became a target for other abusers, one after another, right up to the time she saw me. Dissociation, which had started at age three, continued into adulthood.

Beginning when Ruth was 17, her most damaging abuser terrorized her through both psychological manipulation and physical torture. Pretending to be a therapist, he programed her using hypnosis. This created an alter who was pathologically attached to him. Ruth was programmed with post-hypnotic suggestions to keep coming back to him for years.

Sexual abuse caused a splitting of consciousness in this lonely, sensitive girl, which began a chain reaction of further dissociative responses. This splitting of consciousness has a functional ingenuity: Since only one part of the consciousness faces the overwhelming trauma, other parts are spared. The success of this strategy invites that splitting to become the default response to subsequent stresses, especially when similar stresses occur on an ongoing basis.

There were many alters that had developed by the time Ruth saw me. These included alters who felt unclean, those who felt that she deserved the punishment, and those who commanded her to mutilate herself.

Development of a Complex Multiplicity System

As in all DID patients, each alter functions to fulfill a specific need of the system. Ruth had many simple alters, fragments created in response to one specific traumatic event or life issue. Putnam suggests the more traumatized a patient has been as a child, the more alters or personalities are created in the patient's system.[19] The usual number of alters in a single patient ranges from 8 to 13, but can reach to hundreds. This latter situation is what I later found to be the case for Ruth. When there are hundreds, most of them manifest as fragments of personalities rather than as a personality capable of managing a day-to-day life.[20]

[19]Putnam, F. Diagnosis and Treatment of Multiple Personality Disorders. The Guildford Press. New York, NY. 1989, page 123.

[20]I do not distinguish between alters that are capable of executive function and personality fragments which lack the depth and breadth of a complete personality, having only a limited range of affects, behaviours and life history. My view is that there is no clear distinction between the two groups as their capacities appear to spread across a spectrum. I refer to all such dissociated parts as "alters." See also Putnam's text book, reference 20, p 104.

Ruth initially seemed to have 17 fragments, then 34. Later she found more and more until, by the time she left me, she had found more than 100. Ruth told me emphatically that her alters were not created during therapy.

Although Ruth discovered more and more alters as time went on, she did not get confused about their identities. Indeed, she seemed to have a remarkable ability to maintain clarity about these alters. She distinctly remembered that when she was raped at the age of seven, four parts were split off to handle the horror. This is an example of the fluidity of the dissociative response in that several alters can be involved in holding/managing the memory of one major traumatic event.

Ruth explained how one alter was full of self-disgust, calling herself "filth, trash, with no redeeming features..." Most of the alters freely talked to Ruth, but others sometimes communicated in writing. They each had their own handwriting, which was quite unmistakable and consistent. I have checked and compared the handwriting of a few alters from whom I had received letters two years apart. The handwritings remained unchanged over the years.

Ruth's alters varied greatly in their complexity. As noted, some were simple fragments that appeared to have been created to hold a single emotion of debasement and disgust. Others were more fully developed alters with highly discrete states of consciousness. They were quite capable of executive level functioning.

While the host in many other DID patients is unaware of the existence of alters, Ruth was aware that she had alters from the very beginning. Nevertheless, she had no idea how to handle their excessive emotionality. In particular, she had no idea how to deal with the alter who kept cutting into her arms. There was a risk that this alter could become dangerously out of control. On an ongoing basis, many alters who were suffering from PTSD were threatening to end their own lives or to join the devil. Others complained about the intrusion of terrifying memories.

Despite the outward calm that Ruth exhibited, her inner world was filled with numerous battling factions. Many had quite different world views and allegiances. In particular, some believed they belonged to God while others believed they belonged to the biblical Satan.

The Beginning of Therapy

The first encounter between a patient and a therapist is an important event for both. Its tone often determines the outcome of subsequent therapy. The patient appraises the therapist as much as the other way around. Much of the communication between therapist and patient is non-verbal.

Ruth had traveled hundreds of kilometers to see me, a therapist she had never met. Our interview was part of my daily routine. If she were to decide to take me as her therapist for an undetermined length of time, it would mean that she would have to uproot her entire life and move to a new city.

After our two initial meetings, Ruth calmly said that she had chosen me as her psychiatrist. She was ready to make arrangements to move to Vancouver for ongoing therapy. I was impressed with the quiet strength and determination I saw in this young mother. She had fully utilized her time in my office to give me an almost complete history. Such an encounter with a new patient is rare.

While Ruth had seen numerous doctors and psychiatrists, she had never revealed her history of abuse to anyone until responding to the police officer investigating her principal abuser. She had never revealed her symptoms of multiplicity to anyone.

This is an important point. Perhaps the past assessment interviews had been so staged that there was no chance to reveal these significant traumatic experiences. It is possible that the interview environments were such that she never felt safe enough to do so. Perhaps she had revealed her symptoms and history but they were ignored. It is also possible that interviewers who had heard about the inner voices were unable to see anything other than psychosis and depression.

Although Ruth had finally spoken to a counselor and police officer about her childhood abuse, her words had not resulted in any healing. The police did not feel Ruth's memory was stable enough to enable them to press charges against her abuser. However, in speaking about the abuse at last, she was quite vulnerable and therefore even more subject to the risk of re-traumatization as a result. Merely speaking about the abuse did not help. Debriefing in this way, without proper therapeutic support, did indeed cause re-traumatization.

This helps to explain why patients do not speak out more directly against childhood abusers. Their memories are usually hazy and too unstable to withstand interrogation or courtroom pressure. To the abused, this can only mean that when they tell their personal history of abuse they are not going to be fundamentally believed. This is a vicious dynamic that abusers make use of.

My aim in therapy was to help Ruth handle her multiplicity and process her past trauma. I needed to understand how Ruth's alters functioned as well as how they interfered with and impaired her day-to-day life. While respecting the alters and the roles they played in enabling Ruth to survive the abuse, I had only a limited interest in their lives.

Similarly, I was not interested in the details of her abuse. Neither the method of torture experienced by Ruth, nor the extent of the deviancy of the sexual abuse, was key to her healing from the trauma. The most immediate issue was to deal with the PTSD symptoms of several alters who were bearing heavy loads of unprocessed raw trauma. Many of these wanted only to end the misery of their living hell.

Approaching the Multiplicity

One need not know exactly how many alters any given patient may have, just whether any alters have suicidal, self-destructive or antagonistic agendas. Antagonistic agendas can be dangerous as well as cause disharmony in the group. So long as the alters work as a coordinated team, it does not matter if there are 5 or 500 members in the system.

Although much of the writing on DID suggests that the goal of therapy is to integrate the alters into a unitary personality, that was never my goal. My approach was to help them become, as Putnam recommends, a full functioning unit. If the alters are fused into one personality, there is the risk that without their main defense—disassociation—integrated patients may lack sufficient protection against the ordinary stresses of life, and thus subject to splitting again in the future. This is particularly a risk should a subsequent stressor have anything in common, by word, deed or other trigger, with prior traumas.

In order to facilitate communication with the alters, I asked Ruth to find a way to list the alters of her inner world. I suggested, without giving it much thought, assigning them a number because she would pretty soon run out of letters in the alphabet. She ended with her preliminary list of 34, labeling them numerically with a brief description of each. We quickly found that it was not easy to refer to each as a number. Soon all were assigned names by Ruth. It was easier and more meaningful for both of us to remember a name rather than a number.

In Ruth, the alters were mostly aware of each other, organized in different camps. Initially, there was a group of very distressed alters carrying the raw emotion of terror. These were suffering from flashbacks of that emotion, while others remembered more details of the abuses. Because I could give Ruth only three or four hours a week, a group of helpers among the alters quickly developed as my co-therapists. These had the advantage of being available 24/7.

With few exceptions, successful DID therapy necessarily involves direct dialogue between alters and the therapist. There is no doubt that the traumatic experiences the alters hold need to be processed. Further, individual alters may have numerous issues to be dealt with. There is also bound to be some in-fighting and conflict among them. They need to be taught to live together in harmony and cooperation.

After explaining the condition of DID in general, I asked Ruth to interview each of the alters and use those interviews to introduce her or him to me. Therapy began with the host bringing written notes from home. These notes were verbatim transcripts of the interviewer's questioning of a few of the alters, along with their answers. Some of Ruth's original writings are set forth below, copied word for word from her interview worksheets. These writings were brought into one of the early sessions of therapy.

Alter #1

Ruth: "Can you tell me about yourself and how you feel?"

"I am Pamela. I am Satan's own child and yet in another sense I am also his wife. He loves me and I love him; and he just makes me feel more complete and in control. God's people always hurt me, and I don't like your God. I was made for Satan; I'm his and he's mine. I am obligated to him in every way, so I may as well be happy about it, because we're bound together forever. And I love the sexual pleasure and the power he gives me."

Alter #2

Ruth: "Can you tell me your name and why you enjoy and want physical pain?

"I am Glenda. I was made through the suffering of much pain and agonies, especially physical pain. It is me that had to be the one to take the pain inflicted on us. I don't know any other way of life, but to be in physical pain most or all of the times (sic); and I have come to accept it and want it because nothing else feels normal."

Ruth "Does the pain not hurt you?"

"No. Most of the time I hardly feel it at all, unless it is extremely tortuous (sic), then I do a little bit. But when it is absent for a very long period of time, I feel incomplete and half missing. That is when I have to make some type of pain and discomfort on myself so I can at least be whole and function normally, or else I am lost."

Alter #3

"I hate your family! I hate your family! I hate them and don't want to see them again. They hate me. They hate you. They hate all of us. And will be so pleased and relieved if they would never see us again. They don't care if we're homeless, naked, and penniless or whatever the crisis may be. Their aim in life is to nose into my business, rip our life apart and do whatever possible to make life difficult and distressing. They don't care if we're stuck out here in the middle of nowhere without friends and money, and mechanic bills of $200 or $300. All they do is judge criticize and give their useless ignorant remedies for our trouble which they say is all imagination. I hate your family and never want to see them again."

Alter #4

Ruth: *"What is your name and why do you slash, gash, and make blood flow?"*

"My name is Kerry. I am full of guilt sin and blame; and can never do what is right. I deserve to be punished, to feel extreme pain and I am not worth my blood. My entire life I hate because I am so bad, vile and defiled. I am angry at my wickedness which so many people in this world tell me about in all their assumptions, judging and condemnations. Severe punishment and torture is the best I deserve, and it's my job and goal to give that punishment. The pain and

blood feel and look so great, and I don't care what it does to me, as long as these two are there."

Ruth "Is there no other way to vent your anger and self-hate?".......

This went on for two to three pages in different handwritings for each distinct alter. The ages and functions of some of them are listed below to give a glimpse of Ruth's inner world:

Pamela age 17 Belongs to Satan, wedded to the Devil.

Kerry   age 17 Self-mutilation: Preoccupied with pain, blood and punishment.

Grave   age 8 Sexually abused, feels bad & dirty.

Glenda age ? Holding memory of physical torture, cannot function without pain.

Jeff   age ? Protector/Self-sacrificing; would do anything to protect.

Joyce   age 3 Aversion to family; feels very angry with the family.

Sally   age 15 Suicidal, feels hopeless and worthless; programmed to suicide.

Jane   age 10 Organizer, gives direction, logical. She is a friend and a helper.

Mary   age 16 Extreme mistrustful, terrified of being shot dead. Hates guns

Michelle age 7 Mute, was gagged and repeatedly
raped. Terrified of males. Feels dirty.

Each of the 34 alters known at that time had
individual functions. Their ages ranged from 3 to 17. I do
not know how she kept track of them all before they were
given names, however, it was clear that they were readily
identifiable within the system.

During later sessions, there was a great deal of
repetition of the same themes by these alters. One must be
extra patient with alters repeating a theme. I was confident
that if they needed to repeat themselves, it meant that they
needed such repetition for healing.

Child alters think, feel, speak, and sometimes write,
as young children. This is how they see themselves,
regardless of their chronological age. The therapist must
refrain from judging or treating them as adults.

When alters emerge, therapy should pay full
attention to them because they need that full attention to
heal. Alters holding traumatic memory have been waiting
for someone to listen, console, and comfort them. With
child alters in particular, this is necessary before they can
get past the trauma and heal their wound. One would not
ignore a fallen, crying child for fear of promoting
dependency. Carefully attending to the wound and uttering
words of comfort would be far more appropriate. This
analogy should be kept in mind when engaging child alters
who appear in pain.

Each time Ruth brought in interview transcripts, I
read them aloud. In doing so, I addressed the alters who
wrote the words. At the same time, I told the system that I
expected all the others to be listening. In this way, I used

the direct communication with some alters to extend an invitation to other alters that might need to express something in order to process trauma. Such direct individual contact helped each alter with whom I spoke to develop a therapeutic alliance with me. Simultaneously, it offered a bridge to those that might still be uncertain about trusting me. Most alters were highly receptive to my support and encouragement.

It is critical to be as patient as possible when speaking with alters who initially react to the therapist with suspicion or fear. With patience, I won the trust of those alters that were antagonistic to me. Those with self-destructive urges mellowed, and their exaggerated emotions became milder. Eventually, there remained only a few stubborn ones. These alters resisted change and required more intensive work. With some gentle guidance, understanding, and empathy, they all eventually changed. Their changes reassured me that I was on the right track.

Connecting individually with each alter that required my attention continued for two and half years with very little deviation from the routine. It was impossible to approach every single alter because there were simply too many of them. In speaking with one in need of direct therapeutic intervention, I always framed my communication so as to include all of them as a group. Like speaking to a large audience, I aimed to communicate so that each of those listening felt that they were receiving an individually targeted message. In this way, therapy benefiting one had a positive impact on others – particularly those with memories of similar traumas.

In accordance with my emphasis on the need for cooperation and communication, as well as honoring and supporting one another, the system of alters gradually evolved. They did not integrate into a single unified personality, but instead became a fully functional coalition. While the system and individual alters likely had experienced negative undivided attention from the abusers, they had never experienced *positive* undivided attention from another human being. The impact of therapeutic attention, for even just a few minutes, was a powerful catalyst to initiate change. This demonstrated the power of applying genuine psychotherapy in the context of a correct diagnosis.

Processing the Past Trauma

In encouraging alters to cooperate with one another as they worked toward a common goal of recovery, my therapeutic goal was to help Ruth process the internalized trauma from her abusers. As therapy progressed, Ruth recalled graphic details of her former traumas.

These Ruth's recollections were extremely disturbing. When a patient expresses such difficult recollections, one must listen to the information calmly. One must not prod the patient for disclosure. Neither encourage nor discourage the patient's talking about the details of the abuse. Simply be one-pointed in listening to the details brought up by the alters in therapeutic acknowledgment of their pain. With respect to the patient's pain in remembering, the therapist is a compassionate witness by proxy; assisting her in the here-and-now as the there-and-then no longer exists. This one-pointed deep listening supports healing.

Ruth brought me pages of interview notes and journals, as well as drawings, poems, and many letters written to me. Some were letters from alters, and some were from Ruth, the host. Sometimes Ruth acted as a go-between for certain very timid alters. These had something they had to say but needed some encouragement from me to say it. They had never been acknowledged, never had a chance to relate to someone who was not judgmental. The therapeutic value in giving them the opportunity to speak in this context to someone patient and receptive enough to really listen was immense.

Considering her life at this juncture, Ruth had to be totally genuine and serious in her inner work of healing to accomplish the goal of recovering her children. She had moved to a new and unfamiliar city with little outside support. Her determination and courage was phenomenal. Those qualities, along with the correct diagnosis and a proper therapeutic approach helped her to process past traumas. Meanwhile, the alters were treated with compassion, resulting in them healing, one after another.

Progress in Recovery: The Return of her Children

With exemplary determination and efficiency, Ruth managed not only her work in therapy, but also linked up with social assistance. She was able to find housing, set up a household, and connect with a church. Six months into therapy, she felt well enough to look after her own children and longed for them to be returned to her care.

I asked each of the alters to write me a few lines about having the children back. I asked if they knew of any reason that I should be concerned for the safety of the boys. I was surprised that they all supported the return of the children, including the most negative ones. They all assured me that the boys would be safe. On that basis, I wrote a letter to her lawyer expressing my support for their return.

Ruth's retrieval of her children was legally straightforward and uneventful as she had never signed a consent form to give them away. Her Legal Aid lawyer simply wrote a letter to the American relatives, directing them to return the children to their mother. The lawyer warned that if they failed to comply, the FBI would be informed and a charge of kidnapping would follow.

On the designated date, the children were returned. They arrived with many members of Ruth's family from different parts of Canada. They all gathered in my small office. I saw many angry faces, and the air was thick with hostility. They demanded to know how I could make such an irresponsible decision as to allow Ruth, with her long history of suicide attempts and prolonged hospitalizations, to take back her two sons.

The force of their anger gave me a hint of the intensity of the criticism and rejection Ruth had endured throughout her life. The family members did not understand mental disorders in general, and certainly would not have understood DID. As a result, they were able to see only the negative aspects of Ruth's behavior. On that basis, I believed that their concern for the boys' safety was genuine. Despite the hostility, Ruth stood up calmly and confidently to the scowling family members.

As for me, I was a natural target for them. Ruth's mother started drilling me on religion, speaking amidst the clamor of more than a dozen voices. For her, determining my suitability as a therapist was based on me passing her test of Christian faith and beliefs. I can't imagine what the outcome would have been if I had been a Jew, a Buddhist or a Muslim.

Ruth and her two boys settled into a new apartment complex. Occasionally, she brought them with her to my office. The boys looked clean, happy and well cared for. While Ruth was in therapy with me, the boys interacted cheerfully with my secretary, who always spoke with them. They were kept busy drawing with crayons.

Ruth had begun to make a few friends. She was confident enough to invite them to her home for a roast chicken dinner, homemade bread, and cheesecake. On another occasion, she volunteered to provide cookies for an open house event in her apartment complex. She was thriving and happy with her new life.

Clash of Values with her Family

Despite this positive turn of events, Ruth continued to harbor rage and hatred towards her family in general as well as her mother and some siblings in particular. Indeed, there were good reasons for her to feel this way, both past and present. She received letters from various members of the family criticizing her, judging her, and disagreeing with her decision to leave home and seek therapy with someone of her own choice.

Hardly anyone in that community regarded psychiatry as appropriate help for Ruth. They saw her illness as a spiritual failure, not the result of trauma or DID. On one occasion, her mother told Ruth over the phone that she was not suffering from DID. "It was Satan putting the demons inside you!" she cried. In a clear, even tone, Ruth replied, "If you love me, you should be grateful that my mind allowed these splits rather than giving Satan all the credit that I am still alive. If my mind had not split, I would not be alive to tell the tale."

The head of her church added to the furor, instigating and loudly perpetuating the denial of DID. He also pressured Ruth to reconcile with her estranged abusive husband.

The Road to Healing

When Ruth first saw me, her arms were covered with years of self-inflicted scarring. In therapy, I did not focus on her self-mutilation. I did not want to divert attention and time from the core issue: the task of healing psychological wounds. She excused herself once while in my office, interrupting a session to cut herself in the washroom. I only asked twice about the cutting; at the beginning of therapy and at the end. I was confident that if the therapy was helping her, the cutting behavior would eventually diminish.

The course of therapy for Ruth meant that decisions had to be made given that there were so many alters and issues to heal. The time frame of two and a half years was too short to be divided among what I later learned to be hundreds of alters. I allowed the system to determine the priorities and order of alters to engage.

Perhaps I could have tried to deal directly with the cutter or cutters, but I relied on the resourcefulness and survival capacity of the system for self-protection. I trusted that one of her inner protector alters would jump out to take charge if Ruth got close to dangerously harming herself. I was confident that Ruth was so well motivated and determined to get better, that she would pull through.

Sure enough, over the course of two and half years, her cutting behavior went from several cuttings each day to once a month or less.

Once she started attending psychotherapy regularly, Ruth was no longer depressed. She was full of energy and had a sense of purpose. This was especially true after the return of the boys. She efficiently located pre-schools and day-care for them. I did not believe she needed medication for depression so I proceeded to wean her off the previously prescribed high dose of antidepressant. This was completed uneventfully. I also consulted her neurologist, and successfully withdrew the anti-convulsant medication that she had been taking almost her entire life.

On two separate occasions during the course of therapy, through checking long distance charges on her telephone bill, the host learned that one of the alters was making phone calls to a former abuser. Around each of those times, that alter took over and put the children in the back seat of the car. She then drove north to be reunited with "Satan." Fortunately, the car rides were cut short when another alter, likely the "protector," took over after about 160 kilometers of driving. She turned the car around and brought the children safely home.

One might question how Ruth, or any other victim of abuse, could see an abuser as a lover. Apart from any hypnotic influence, he was at least some human contact for this individual who'd never had a non-abusive relationships within her family or anywhere else. A key component to this analysis is that the nature of her dissociation also meant that the particular alter who saw the abuser as her lover remembered nothing about his cruelty and torturing of Ruth.

Paradoxically, the religious upbringing that was so entwined with her suffering also contributed to her healing. In essence, the alters were split between two camps; between Good (Jesus) and Evil (Satan). As the alters in one camp fought with the alters in the other camp, Ruth prayed continuously for support and guidance from God.

The breakthrough came when the patient, without my instigation, ingeniously assigned an alter that was a powerful preacher and healer within her inner family to deal with this problem of having followers of Satan inside. Eventually, Ruth reported that many of those belonging to Satan were converted by the powerful preacher. Much therapy can be accomplished through an alter who is an inner helper.

Ruth was steadfast in her faith. I am convinced that without this deep faith, Ruth would have succumbed to the tremendous forces of despair that had visited her throughout years of alienation. On one occasion, she asked me to call her at a time of my convenience. There was a specific purpose: to encourage one alter who was on the verge of a "conversion." This most pessimistic and negative alter, who "had surrendered to Satan", was close to being "converted to Christ" because of the efforts of the preacher alter. Ruth believed that the conversion of this alter was critical to overcoming the strongest obstructive force against healing and recovery. Overcoming such forces during a healing process involving alters is profound both in its intent and effect.

The provincial College of Physicians specifically forbids doctors to engage in religious matters during therapy sessions. Our license is for medical practice, not for preaching. It was important to maintain that boundary while at the same time supporting the alter that provided this function internally. I did call Ruth. In that call, I did not preach to the negative alter, but I did indeed heartily support the preacher alter's efforts in this context.

Despite the intensity and deep involvement in time and energy on my part, Ruth was careful not to become unduly dependent on me. She only called me outside therapy sessions on that one occasion. My secretary, who had social work training, did much supportive work helping Ruth in the move that enabled her to see me in therapy.

Therapeutic Outcome

At the outset, I had asked Ruth to commit to the program of psychotherapy with the stipulation that she would not return to her abusive husband, nor have any romantic attachments to anyone, until she finished therapy. She honored her commitment for two and half years. At that point, she decided to return to her husband and abruptly terminated therapy. By then, she had made tremendous progress. Years later, she finally broke up with her husband for good.

Over the years, she kept in touch with me through occasional letters to my secretary. Through those letters, I knew that there continued to be marital abuse and other difficulties. Twelve years later, she invited me to visit her if I happened to be in the province where she now lived. When I went east on unrelated matters, I decided to take a side trip to see her.

When I met with her, she let me know what had happened since terminating therapy with me. Upon returning to her community and abusive husband, she continued to receive harsh criticism from the church. The head of the church, who had pressured her to return to her sadistic husband, still strongly disputed the diagnosis of DID. However, at last mentally and physically well, able to care for her children on her own, Ruth left her husband and her church for good, moving to a congenial and supportive Christian community in another province.

She no longer needed to take any psychiatric medication or to contact any mental health personnel, though she had received some assistance from a few counselors in her new Christian community. Slowly, she had even built a relationship with her mother and siblings.

Ruth told me that the total number of alters was at least 475. She again stressed that none were created during therapy. Now healthy, all of the alters worked together as a unified functioning team. Ruth gave me a thank-you card crammed with signatures, all in different handwritings. I still recognized some of the alters' handwritings after more than a decade.

I met the elders in her Christian community. They were supportive of Ruth, and thankful for what we accomplished in therapy. Despite everything she faced, Ruth was able to triumph against all odds.

Ruth was unique in many ways. Despite all the pessimism surrounding her and contrary to the usual pattern, the host was highly motivated and energetically sought treatment. Ruth's strong faith in God gave her an unusual quiet strength. Furthermore, she was totally focused on getting well. Her critical mind was active and alert. After careful evaluation, she followed my instructions very conscientiously, but not blindly.

Ruth responded dramatically to therapeutic intervention, unlike many other traumatized patients. I have never met such a compliant and appreciative patient, and I believe the positive outcome in this therapy was due to her strong religious faith. To her, I was just an "instrument of God" to help her get better.

The key point here is to understand the importance of working with the strengths of a patient, religious or otherwise. Therapy should not deny the fact that religious faith can play an extremely important role in some patients' healing.

Financial Considerations of Ruth's Treatment

Ruth's intensive treatment of three to four hours a week for two and a half years was unusual when compared to my norm, or to the practice of my peers. The high number of hours I was billing caught the attention of the medical insurance plan provider. I received a letter threatening to limit the number of hours allowed per week for Ruth's psychotherapy. In response, I simply pointed out Ruth's medical expenses for the 12 months before she began seeing me as compared with the medical expenses for the 12 months after beginning psycho-therapy with me.

During her therapy with me, she neither consulted any other mental health professional nor did she visit any hospital emergency department. In addition, all her expensive psychiatric medications had gradually been discontinued. As Ruth was on social assistance, even the medication costs were borne by the public. During Ruth's five month hospital confinement before seeing me, the cost of an in-patient stay in a general hospital, not counting doctor's consultation and attendance fees, medications and other expenses, was around $800 per day. After receiving my letter, the medical providers assured me that weekly hours of therapy would not be restricted for this patient.

I was gratified to receive this confirmation that the work I had done with Ruth had tangible benefits for society at large. I was also grateful that our British Columbia medical insurance plan (MSP) was flexible enough to consider cases on an individual basis.

The correct diagnosis and treatment of Ruth's illness, DID, put a stop to the useless drain of manpower, medical resources, medication costs, hospital bed occupancy, psychiatric consultation fees and other social services, for at least the next 17 years. It is hard to put a number in dollars and cents to the equation, but the savings are no doubt extraordinary. My response to the medical plan providers was limited to only the last 12 months of medical expenses, not the expenses borne by society going back two decades. What cannot be calculated is the deliverance from suffering of a young mother and her children, returning to them the possibility of a hopeful future.

Chronic psychiatric disability and management of same is a major factor in the increasing demand for psychiatric and social services. It is a hole in the pocket of the public purse. Ruth's prior pattern of utilizing health care services is an example of what is now termed a "super-user." According to the US Agency for Healthcare Research and Quality, super-users constitute 1% of the population but account for 21% of healthcare costs.[21]

Ruth is not the only misdiagnosed DID super-user in

---

[21]Out of a $1.3 trillion budget according to Statistical brief #421 http://meps.ahrq.gov/mepsweb/data_files/publications/st421/stat421.shtml

the health care system. Other case histories discussed here, and other patients I have seen, would also be classified as super-users. Correct diagnoses can plug this hole, allowing precious financial resources to be applied to society's many other needs.

Ruth's Epilogue

I sent Ruth the initial draft of this chapter with an invitation for her to comment, and to verify the information it contains. In March 2013, I got the following note from her, which included publication permission:

> *After my first appointment with Dr. David Yeung on June 16, 1996, I felt angry at having the D.I.D. label put on me, due to the terror of additional rejection and ostracization from family and church. However, in the second appointment he began to instruct me about the importance of validating each fragmented piece of me. It was then that something akin to hope began to burst forth from the inner depths of unspeakable anguish and chaos, amid the constant hundreds of opinions within. Individual parts of me took notice in amazement that some Professional would take the time to acknowledge their specific load of agony! Though trust was hard to come by due to years of abuse, "this Doctor was different" and was making a safe place for everyone to show up, be themselves, and/or speak. When the braver inner individuals spoke directly to "this different Doctor" in safety, many others surged forward to observe the miracle – eventually daring to be heard also.*

> *My previous anger re: diagnosis soon turned to*

abundant thanksgiving to God for finally sending someone who truly understood the inner broken pieces, and who desired to help without judgment!

The things written herein about Ruth's experiences and journey to hope, help and healing are authentic and true. Had I not received the correct diagnosis when I did, and received such miraculous assistance, it is most probable that I would not have survived much longer the after-effects and programming of the years of abuse, while struggling all alone. My counselors 6 years later repeatedly affirmed, "If Dr. D. Yeung had not laid the foundation with the correct diagnosis and how to deal with the individual parts, we would not have been able to truly help you." Praise be to God!

In Gratitude, Ruth

13 march 2013

More than 17 years after Ruth first stepped into my office in 1996, she again wrote to me that she was busy managing a website introducing books to help abuse survivors, especially for people with DID. Further, she has been invited by a publisher to write a "devotional book for survivors" of physical, emotional, and sexual abuse.

Ruth's story is an inspiring living testimony for the power of faith and the profundity of the human spirit. For the therapist, it demonstrates that treatment of DID has the possibility of unimaginable reward.

Therapeutic Keys

The DID response results from trauma that most people simply cannot imagine and that response enables the individual to survive the trauma. Accessing the insight and skills of the dissociative parts requires interpreting their needs and supporting their efforts to effect healing. The therapist can only appreciate the possibilities by directly engaging the alters and understanding their conduct in context.

Therapists must keep in mind that the environment that produced, acquiesced in, or actively supported trauma may be an ongoing influence on the patient, continuing the trauma. When there is a mix of flashbacks as well as continuing current impacts from that environment, the patient needs support both in dealing with flashbacks as well as establishing current boundaries of protection.

Chapter 6 Melanie – The Most Unwanted

Melanie is an example of a not uncommon phenomenon: an unpopular patient on the Emergency ward who is equally unpopular in the psychiatric ward. She had a history of multiple admissions, multiple complaints and appeared to be an angry person. Her medical record revealed diagnoses carrying pejorative meanings that often stigmatize a patient. For example, any patient who has been diagnosed with borderline personality disorder (BPD), such as Melanie, is bound to elicit some negative response from the treatment team. Abuse of narcotics and alcohol was also included on her chart.

BPD is a descriptive term denoting a patient whose essential features are a pattern of marked impulsivity and instability of affects, interpersonal relationships, and self-image. The pattern is present by early adulthood and occurs in a variety of contexts. Other symptoms may include intense fears of abandonment as well as intense anger and irritability. The reasons for such fears and angers are difficult for others to understand. A description like BPD, and in a similar way depression, can be a smoke screen hiding the core pathology of trauma and dissociation. The harmful resulting reactions of mental health workers is called negative counter-transference. These reactions diminish the chance of the patient receiving satisfactory treatment.

It was just this constellation of negativity that surrounded Melanie in the health care system,[22] as she was considered, essentially, a psychiatric "hot potato." Her

---

[22]The equivalent BPD diagnosis in ICD 10 is "emotional unstable personality." This is again a descriptive term for certain character faults rather than a diagnostic label. These descriptive terms have become corrupted into terms of stigmatization.

previous treatment on the ward was full of negative experiences for both her and the treatment team.

Melanie's Story

Melanie was 17 when I first met her. She was lying on a stretcher in the over-flowing emergency ward of the hospital one evening when I was on-call. She was in a bad mood, suffering from multiple physical problems and post-motor vehicle accident ("MVA") pain. Melanie was depressed and suicidal. In short, she had problems physically, socially and psychologically.

Melanie told me that she hated hospitals and doctors - especially psychiatrists. Such an initial presentation was hardly conducive to a positive therapeutic alliance. The hospital file that came with her included a long list of assorted problems: recurrent nightmares, hearing voices creating internal chaos, fibromyalgia, ulcerative colitis, post-MVA with multiple aches and pains, as well as alcohol and narcotics abuse.

Her personal history involved multiple intra-family sexual and physical abuse beginning in early childhood. Both parents had committed suicide, and there were many boarding home placements, the number of which she could not recall. She told me all these things in anger. Sensing a fighting spirit in her, I decided to take her on as a patient and asked her to see me in my office. I discharged her from the hospital as she was unlikely to do well in the psychiatric ward. It is unlikely that anyone with such a mixture of diagnoses and descriptions would make progress toward healing in that environment.

Melanie came from an aboriginal community where

social breakdown had occurred at every level. Like so many aboriginal communities, after being robbed of their traditions and collective pride by the dominant culture, Melanie's had been left empty and disorganized. One result was that it was filled with rampant sexual abuse. Associated with the sexual abuse was the unholy triad of substance abuse (alcoholism and narcotics), prostitution and suicide. Girls running away from such communities generally congregate in the inner city to form a subculture characterized by poverty and degradation.

Melanie never experienced the sense of safety and security that children require in the early stages of psychosocial development in order to mature emotionally. Persons who have been abused in early life develop fine antennae attuned to the slightest negative feelings from anyone, and a vicious cycle may become established. Even the normally healing environment of a hospital may become another place of rejection, a confirmation of both conscious and unconscious expectations of hostility. As with Melanie's peers, a history of rejection had turned into an expectation of rejection. Most people Melanie had encountered in life had confirmed this expectation.

It would take a few more meetings like this initial contact at the Emergency Ward before Melanie began coming, fairly regularly, to my office for psychotherapy. She continued to be depressed and suicidal, and in lingering pain from car accidents. She was so jumpy that it was hard not to absorb some of her nervous energy. She'd already had extensive involvement with doctors, lawyers, social workers, and counselors. In the beginning, there appeared to be no hope of improvement on any front.

Something overrode my initial prejudice toward this young girl, who had clearly been forced to grow up too fast.

I admired her combative, fighting spirit. After our connection was firmly established, I decided to treat her as one suffering from borderline personality disorder even though, then and now, BPD suggests a negative prognosis. This was before Linehan's contribution[23] to this topic was generally acknowledged.

In addition to her drug, depression, social and physical problems, she manifested many dissociative features. I noted the dissociative features but refrained, as yet, from delving into the possibility of DID.

A Reluctant Diagnosis of DID

Melanie's life was unsettled. There were intervals when she would cancel an appointment and be out of contact for a few months at a time. As a result, therapy sessions over the ensuing years were clustered sporadically. Both of us were strangely persistent. Surprisingly, Melanie never missed an appointment. I was always re-connected with her when she landed in the local hospital emergency room.

Five years after our first encounter, I was presented with ten dissociated parts inside her. Three of them appeared during one session in my office. I had been trying to avoid the diagnosis of DID as I was not keen to add yet another diagnostic label with negative connotations to her thick medical record.

---

[23]Marsha Linehan, the originator of Dialectical Behavior Therapy, has written and taught extensively on BPD. She has offered the most effective treatment to date for this condition. People with BPD often engage in idealization and devaluation of others, alternating between high positive regard and great disappointment. Self-mutilation and suicidal behaviors are common in BPD.

The appearance of the alters signaled the level of disturbance that was playing out in her life, and that is where I put the therapeutic focus. While I did not ignore the alters, from then on I spoke to Melanie while always being mindful of their presence. I did not pursue engaging the alters in therapy directly because, at the time, the alters did not appear to be in great conflict. Therefore, engaging them directly at that point was unnecessary. In retrospect, had I actively engaged the alters in therapy the outcome might have been more positive.

Emotional and Practical Therapeutic Support

I kept in touch with Melanie for ten years. I wanted her to understand that I was there for the long haul. I hoped that the continuity of our relationship, and the knowledge that I was reliable, would help foster some of the trust that had been so sorely lacking in her childhood. Since her primary symptoms were intense fearfulness and recurrent nightmares, I focused on ways to help her feel safe in the present moment.

Realizing the magnitude of unprocessed traumatic material she carried, I taught her relaxation techniques. She learned to create a calm imaginary safe place in which to retreat, using visual imagery and self-suggestion. I also practiced some hypnotic suggestion to comfort the traumatized inner child, helping her to imagine that the older and more mature Melanie could comfort and console the waif-like child inside. These techniques of self-soothing, involving guided visualization, can empower a traumatized patient.

In her self-created safe place, Melanie was able to

rest and recharge. It was a place of calm where she was neither emotionally numb nor swept away by overwhelming feelings. Melanie needed to internalize a sense of her intrinsic value, something she did not learn at a crucial early stage of development. What she needed, like all of us, was nurturing non-judgmental love.

These are tried and true methods for helping those who were neglected or abused when they were children. They are a kind of corrective re-parenting by the therapist. When using these methods, therapists must be cautioned to maintain their perspective. A therapist who gets over-involved may become depleted. Compassion fatigue and the blurring of boundaries is not an uncommon result among dedicated therapists. A patient who has begun to count on unconditional love from the therapist may get explosively angry when the well seems to have run dry.

Therapists must know themselves well enough to be on sure ground. In a sense, they are modeling a new way of relating for the patient; blending compassionate caring with a certain detachment. It keeps their own feet planted firmly on the ground, whatever storms the patient might go through.

Melanie also needed practical help, as her medical problems and social turmoil were serious distractions to psychotherapeutic progress. I spent much time communicating with social workers and writing letters on her behalf to lawyers, many of whom seemed skeptical about her claims and unsympathetic.

I fought hard to resist an opposing lawyer's request to use her medical records in the court action that followed a motor vehicle accident. There were too many negative comments in the medical records that the lawyer could have used to discredit her. Most importantly, I knew how traumatic it would be for her to have her history of abuse read out in court, and then be attacked by lawyers on the witness stand.

This highlights the potential conflict between the mental health and legal process systems. One must bear in mind that medical records could be read out in a court of law at some future date. They could be used out of context for purposes completely unrelated to and antithetical to therapy. In representing the car insurance company, the lawyer would have just been doing his job to undermine Melanie's credibility. However, in doing so in order to downplay her chronic pain, he would likely have undermined whatever therapeutic progress Melanie might have made then or in the future.

Outcome: A Qualified Success

During our on and off therapy over ten years, Melanie took several steps toward self-improvement. She attended AA (Alcoholics Anonymous) as well as NA (Narcotics Anonymous) meetings, becoming drug-free and alcohol-free two years after she started seeing me. Although it took years, she finally left her boyfriend, whose influence on her was far from positive. After switching jobs a few times, she finally found one that she liked well enough to stay with; working with street kids in a group home. Her work there was highly appreciated.

The social turmoil that had always followed in her wake finally simmered down. Her physical condition improved. In the sessions of later years, she never mentioned symptoms associated with fibromyalgia, ulcerative colitis, or other aches and pain. She also appeared calmer, more in control, and more confident of herself.

In one of the last sessions, she told me that she was not "a multiple" and that there were no alters inside her. As previously noted, this is not an uncommon phenomenon in DID patients. They sometimes recant the history of abuse and deny the multiplicity. With DID, it is often the case that the host wishes to deny the presence and memories of the alters, or simply does not know of them.

There was no need to defend the diagnosis. I had met Melanie's alters, and they had met me. We knew each other. We had developed a therapeutic alliance. The proof was Melanie's strong improvement and well-being.

With Melanie, the focus of my treatment was not her DID. While I used ordinary psychotherapeutic supports, I kept in mind that she was a DID and that the alters were listening when I spoke to her. That was enough to effect improvement. The changes in her, comparing the first 17 years of her life to the next ten, were extensive, deep and positive. She was, relatively speaking, peaceful and stable as well as successful in keeping herself drug and alcohol free.

I characterize the outcome as a qualified success because the DID was not fully treated. Perhaps that is unnecessary as clearly the parts were all working together in a positive and supportive manner. Because the amnestic barrier remained, it is likely that the splitting would become problematic under future stresses that might mimic prior abuse.

Lessons from Melanie Regarding BPD

The work with Melanie left a strong imprint on me. There are patients for whom the diagnostic label of BPD does more harm than good. While the diagnosis in and of itself may be helpful in some contexts, the real pathology of DID can easily be hidden under the shadow of BPD

The negativity that results from receiving a label such as BPD underlies a larger problem with diagnostic labels that we must keep in mind. We cannot do without them, since they point to appropriate treatment methods when coupled with a correct diagnosis. However, labels can sometimes stereotype and stigmatize as well as be given in error. In the face of confusion, mystery, and frustration, it can be tempting to grab at an explanatory label. Nevertheless, therapists must be careful to avoid considering the label more than the person. Behind the label, there is always a suffering human being.

Once again, there is an extraordinary cost to society resulting from incorrect diagnostic labels. Once correctly diagnosed, Melanie's entire therapy involved approximately 125 therapeutic hours. Emergency visits to the hospital and referrals to other medical specialists were greatly reduced as her life was stabilized, again demonstrating the economic value of appropriate non-pharmaceutical psychiatry.

Therapeutic Keys

Some psychiatrists do not consider how childhood traumas may have given rise to symptoms similar to those of BPD. This is an example of how past trauma is frequently played down when considering etiology in mental disorders. As a result, this label may be misapplied to DID patients, whose switching alters present a similar appearance of highly unstable moods. Therapists must learn to distinguish between such unstable moods and appearing alters.

Paying attention to sudden shifts in body language can clarify whether it is simply a mood change or whether an alter has appeared. In the same way, changes in speech patterns, handwritings (when available), and transition indicators such as brief headaches immediately before and after such changes, serve as valuable guideposts. Of course, direct interaction with alters is the key confirmation. In Melanie's case, the alters were not raising problems in therapy. Speaking primarily to the host may be sufficient therapeutic intervention, as long as one keeps in mind that all of the alters are listening.

Borderline Personality Disorder is closely associated with DID, as they often share the same background of childhood trauma.[24] Many DID patients are seen as BPD, but it may be simply that one dominant alter is suffering from BPD. If a different alter comes out at another time showing a very different behavior profile, then the patient will surely but incorrectly be considered a fake. I believe

---

[24]Horevitz and Braun found that 70 percent of patients who had been diagnosed with Multiple Personality Disorder/DID would just as likely, by chart review, meet the criteria for BPD. Horevitz RP, Braun BG. Are multiple personalities borderline? an analysis of 33 cases. Psychiatr Clin North Am. 1984;7:69–87

many DID patients are missed, hidden behind a diagnosis of BPD.

Chapter 7 Victoria - Long Distance Treatment

Out of necessity, Victoria was treated on an out-patient basis, as she was living hundreds of kilometers away. Every session was tailored to promote maximum self-healing, and relied much on the independence, intelligence and resourcefulness of the patient. The therapeutic progress was accomplished with the help of an "inner therapist." Home-work assignments, periodic reviews during in-office visits, and eventually video-taping the home sessions, evolved into a practical therapeutic program.

Although Victoria was a textbook case of MPD, the diagnosis was missed by the five psychiatrists who had seen her during the previous two years. Because she lived some 900 kilometers away from me, and I could not find a local therapist for her, office treatment posed a particular problem. She had no option but to drive all the way to see me for outpatient office visits on a monthly basis during the initial period. Later, the intervals between office visits were spread more widely apart.

We managed to complete therapy in 25 sessions stretched over seven years. Each session required Victoria to make round trip drives of 1,800 kilometers. By cultivating an inner therapist in one alter, it became possible to provide effective treatment while minimizing the number of office sessions.

Her accomplishments in therapy were remarkable. They demonstrate the benefit of directly connecting to the insight and wisdom that alters can provide. One can look at this as having taken a long time; seven years. Alternatively, one can look at this as a relatively brief treatment; taking only 25 sessions.

Victoria was a 46 year old mental health worker who had been employed as a counselor with the local native population in a remote, isolated community in the North. While counseling trauma survivors, she seemed to have "slipped." She began to experience bouts of depression, and was at times suicidal. Before her arrival in my office, I received a letter of introduction from her general practitioner, who referred her to me, and a consultation report from another psychiatrist about her.

The indication was that the onset of her breakdown was the result of overwork with trauma victims. Alternatively, or possibly as a contributing factor, there was the likelihood that working with traumatized children triggered her own early traumatic memories to such a degree that she became disabled. The psychiatrist's report also mentioned dissociative symptoms but did not consider Multiple Personality Disorder as a diagnosis.

Psychiatrists regularly visited that remote area, but they seldom engaged in psychotherapy. Their main function was triage, to check medications, and to prepare consult reports. As a result, Victoria had begun psychotherapy with a social worker who lived 60 km away. The reporting psychiatrist, who did not mention a diagnosis of MPD, was located 150 km away from Victoria's community.

In those previous two years, she had been seen by five psychiatrists and admitted three times to the hospital. Her diagnoses included manic-depressive disorder, borderline personality disorder, PTSD, brief reactive psychosis, and personality disorder characterized as "histrionic and borderline."[25] At one point, when she

---

[25] These are diagnoses that are commonly applied in error to DID patients.

showed no improvement on anti-depressants, ECT was considered. This idea was dropped when she showed some temporary improvement.

The visiting psychiatrists and attending physicians did not know what to do with her. They prescribed anti-psychotic medication and recommended giving her four weeks sick leave. She then came to see me.

The General Practitioner's Introduction

Victoria was sexually abused by her father until the time of her first period. She was also abused by two other members of her immediate family.

She had been home-schooled until the age of ten, and then entered public school. She later attended university, from which she graduated with a BA. She worked for many years in childcare before being employed as a drug and alcohol abuse counselor. Later, she worked for two years as a sexual abuse counselor for traumatized survivors in the native population.

Her family doctor described her as being volatile and emotional. Much of the description was focused on her "out of body" experiences and on "fragmentation." She had flashbacks and "could dissociate."

Victoria had also revealed that the only time she felt okay was when she was working with abuse victims. She "would lose it when she was on her own." She felt she was "fractured" and that "all the parts are scattering about" despite her attempts to gather them. The family doctor's description included the following statements made by Victoria: "fragmentation, fracture, dissociate, all the parts scattering, out of body...." These descriptions were used repeatedly by Victoria in describing herself when she saw me.

First Interview

Victoria told me that she was afraid she might be suffering from MPD. I asked if she had read anything about MPD, and she said no. Just the term, Multiple Personality Disorder, seemed concordant with her experience. For clarity, the terms and expressions in quotes below are those used by Victoria.

Four months ago, while participating in a "kinesthetic workshop" where she was "encouraged to have an out-of-body experience", she had found herself unable to stop crying. After seeing her social worker therapist over the last few months, she realized she was "splitting." Then she said, "When I split, there is an angry part...I am afraid of being taken over...People are afraid of the violent one inside me."

During that very first interview, without prompting, she gave me a rough sketch of some of the "parts" inside her:

1. "Victoria" - the counselor

2. "I am" - the host

3. "She" - the angry part who wanted to kill

4. The "horny one" - young girl who desperately wanted to have sex with her father

5. The "violent one"

6. The "inner therapist"

7. The Others

She did not identify "The Others" who were having flashbacks. I did not rule out the possibility of violent physical abuse in addition to extreme erotic stimulation during the original trauma.

From the assorted diagnoses she had received, the most appropriate was PTSD. However, there was clearly more going on. Without recognizing the clinical states of dissociation disorders, one would be at a loss as to how to treat this patient. Her last psychiatrist described her as psychotic and treated her with anti-psychotic medication. The term psychotic indicates, among other things, that the patient's utterances make no sense. A diagnosis of MPD put her speech into a clearly comprehensible context.

The social worker therapist had mentioned a possible diagnosis of MPD for Victoria. However, the patient did not want to accept it. She was in fact quite scared of being a "Split Personality." I neither confirmed nor denied the diagnosis of MPD when I first saw her. I went on to talk to her and to the alters she had named as if it were the most natural thing in the world. She never questioned me doing so. Her matter-of-fact way of identifying the "parts" clearly suggested that Victoria had no desire to dramatize these alters, but had merely given them names for the purpose of identification.

Looking through the lens of an MPD diagnosis, it is easily understood why Victoria's child alters spoke in their child language, while the "inner therapist" spoke to me like a professional colleague.

Treating Victoria's fragmentation as a psychosis was a mistake. Using anti-psychotic medication might, temporarily, chemically muffle the voices. However, it would not make any difference other than perhaps to confirm further to the alters that neither they nor the pain, fear and damage that they held were acknowledged. Medication had not engendered any healing in those prior years.

Symptomology

Victoria had the full blown multiplicity symptoms of MPD, with alters creating chaos due to in-fighting amongst them. The imminent problem was the presence of the "violent one" and "She." Together, they made a dangerous couple capable of murdering the "horny one" regardless of the fact that it would mean suicide for the host and death for all of the alters.

Victoria warned me that the "angry one" had elicited fear in her family doctor at home. The doctor was well aware of the explosive anger inside threatening to strike. Victoria had alters suffering from severe PTSD flashbacks. These alters were interfering in her everyday life. Other alters were quite depressed, and some alters were strongly attached to the abuser. These latter ones were still craving his love, which provoked the angry alter to erupt in violence.

The Childhood Roots of Victoria's DID

Since her sexual abuse history had already been documented by her doctor, I did not ask any further questions about it. There appeared to be no benefit in going into it unless and until Victoria or an alter raised it. To have raised it on my end would definitely have risked re-traumatization.

Victoria's MPD was the unconscious self-protective strategy to which some child victims of abuse turn. Like MPD, incest was not something talked about in our medical training. However, the failure to discuss incest was not based on a dispute about whether or not it existed: It was an uncomfortable topic that much of society simply refused to look at. I had some insight into the dynamics of this pernicious form of child abuse, as I had quite often seen victims of father-daughter incest in my office.

Older textbooks touched on the topic of father-daughter incest only in passing. It was discussed mainly in the context of social taboos, or when considering the Freudian Oedipal and Electra Complexes. Weinberg[26] reported that the statistical rate of incest conviction in the US was 1.2 per million persons (.00012%) in 1930. This number has been quoted in books for decades, creating a misleading impression that incest is rare. It should be noted that this figure refers to convictions and should not be confused with the statistical rate of incidence, which is substantially higher.

Judith Hermann's seminal 1981 book, *Father-Daughter Incest*, brought the issue into sharp focus. By the 1990s, when I was seeing Victoria, there was more public awareness. A 1988 Finnish study, carried out on 9000 15-

---

[26] Weinberg, S. Kirson (1955) *Incest Behavior*. New York: Citadel Press.

year-old schoolgirls, had found the prevalence of incest to be 2% with biological fathers and 3.7% with step-fathers.[27] Father-daughter incest is and was not as rare as many would like to believe, even today. In my experience, the rate of incest in certain communities is staggeringly high, such as in aboriginal communities suffering the aftermath of cultural genocide.

In Victoria's case, the splitting off of one part of her into a hyper-sexualized young girl-child can be understood by reflecting on the typical etiology of incest abuse. Like other incest victims, Victoria would have had a complex and contradictory emotional response to the abuse. With no resources to resist the authority figure who was abusing her, there would be the experience of an absolute loss of control. Along with fear, pain, hurt, sadness, guilt and shame, she most likely felt a desire for revenge mixed in with an intense longing to please.

When the element of eroticism cannot be blocked out, the young child looks upon the abuser as her lover, creating more shame and guilt. When one event of abuse is completed, children like Victoria must pretend that life goes on normally. The illusion of normalcy continues until the next abuse begins. There is no one in whom it is safe to confide.

There is no doubt incest is among the most malignant and vicious forms of childhood sexual abuse.

---

[27] H Sariola, A Uutela *The Prevalence and Context of Incest Abuse in Finland*. Child Abuse & Neglect 10/1996; 20(9):843-50 DOI:10.1016/0145-2134(96)00072-5

Victoria's Inner World

Among the alters, the most persistent and prominent was the "horny one." Initially, she maintained a high profile. She was frequently out in a very obstructive way, causing embarrassment and difficulty for the host and others. She expressed a continuous need for sex, as if it was a perpetually unsatisfied hunger. Of the reactive parts, the "violent one" and "She" were threatening to act upon their desire to maim and kill the horny one.

These reactive parts initially presented to me as two discreet alters. I suspect they eventually became one as therapy proceeded. Similarly, the initially separated Victoria, the "counselor" and the "inner therapist" appeared to have come together with the common goal of healing the system. Again, there was no benefit in my trying to discriminate amongst similarly presenting alters that were not in conflict.

According to Victoria and her medical records, the only time she was feeling all right was when she was at work. The inner therapist (or therapists) must have been there for years, functioning perfectly in Victoria's work counseling victims of sexual abuse. I was grateful that I could then make valuable use of this system, already in place at the very beginning of the therapy.

The Abuser-Victim-Rescuer Triad

Given Victoria's history of abuse, it is not coincidental that the host, or some alters, would assume the role of the rescuer in working with traumatized children. This was something that she had desperately needed in her own childhood.

In childhood abuse, there is a triad of abuser, victim and rescuer, often linked in curious ways. One who has been abused can have alters that fall into one of the following roles:

Rescuer

Abuser   Victim

An alter will most likely arise repeatedly in the role of a victim. Another alter will likely arise in the role of a rescuer. Finally, there is often an alter that can arise as a perpetrator.[28] Alters can appear in all three roles, even within the same encounter. Further, even when an alter displays in one of those roles, those in the other roles are present and often actively in conflict.

All three roles were found among Victoria's alters. Victoria's angry alter was really an abuser, wanting to kill the hyper-sexualized young child. Victoria was greatly agitated by the battles between the "horny one" and the many alters who wanted to viciously punish, attack and crush this part. Completing the triad, there was an alter fulfilling the role of a rescuer. This alter functioned as a good sexual abuse counselor as well as a good inner-therapist for Victoria's own healing.

---

[28] On abused who then go on to become abusers, see: http://bjp.rcpsych.org/content/179/6/482.full

With respect to the abuser-victim-rescuer triad, the playing out of these roles can also be seen in the therapeutic relationship. This is especially true when therapy takes a wrong turn. Therapists may become the victim with the patient reversing the roles and becoming the rescuer.

Treatment Decision; First Session

Since the patient had come from hundreds of kilometers away, and the referral referenced a risk of suicide, a quick decision was necessary as to whether Victoria was best treated at home or in a hospital setting. Given my experience with DID patients in hospitals, however sick Victoria appeared, it was critical to create a therapeutic alliance that would enable her to return to her home while remaining safe.

During our first session, I offered Victoria my view that working with sexual abuse victims had likely triggered the return of her own traumatic memories in the form of uncontrollable flashbacks. I told her that I believed she had re-awakened the dissociated parts now causing great turmoil in her inner world. This uncontrollable acting out of the alters had made her life overwhelmingly chaotic.

This analysis made sense to her. I then proceeded to give her instructions in how she might regain control and a semblance of orderliness back into her daily life. I gave her exercises to do at home. She listened attentively and made notes. Her critical receptivity to my suggestions gave me hope that she could indeed go home and see me as an outpatient. In my estimation, this was preferable to her being admitted to a hospital or relocating to Vancouver for treatment. I spent the next hour outlining goals:

1. To teach "She" and the "angry one" to accept that while their rage was understandable, they needed to make peace with the horny one. They needed to help her, not kill her. They needed to learn to deal with their intense anger. They also needed to appreciate the simple anatomical fact that they were sharing the same body with the one they wanted to kill.

2. To convince the hyper-sexualized child alter that the past was in the past, and that the father of some 40 years ago was long gone. She had been hyper-stimulated sexually at a completely inappropriate age and place, and in the completely inappropriate context of incest. Of course, she had no idea how to handle the flashbacks of that arousal or the desire for it in the present. Her intense sexual craving was so strong that the energy had to be dissipated in some way. This child alter was not interested in understanding the etiology of the confusion or whether the arousal was appropriate then or now. She simply expressed the absolute need to satisfy her cravings. Therefore, the suggestion was that she be given permission and, in fact, encouraged to masturbate rather than seeking external fulfillment for the unhealthy attachment to her long deceased father. Masturbation was clearly the safest course of action for her.[29]

3. To ground herself as a way to bring her body and mind to a state of equanimity. This involved learning to go to an imaginary place where she could feel safe

---

[29] Jocelyn Elders, former Surgeon General of the United States, was forced to resign following her recommendation of masturbation as part of sex education to avoid spreading HIV/Aids. For Melanie, sexual desire was incredibly dangerous to act upon – not just for the risk of HIV/Aids.

physically. She could learn to feel solidly grounded by using her imagination, picturing her feet growing ten feet down into the ground like the roots of a big tree. It would take a lot of work to accomplish this major therapeutic practice.

Grounding

Victoria was able to use self-healing skills as had been taught to other patients. These included dealing with flashbacks by utilizing some grounding techniques.

The key point is empowering the patient to re-possess her own body. When undergoing uncontrollable flashbacks, patients usually feel a complete loss of power. This happens because the body is hijacked when the traumatic memory takes over physiological processes during the flashbacks.

Grounding teaches the patient to learn once again what it is to feel safe psychologically. There are many such grounding exercises. The term and concept of grounding is borrowed from the study of electricity. It is used in therapy as if everyone knows what it means, but there is no real consensus as to its definition when applied to psychotherapy.

The appropriate analogy is lightning: When lightning strikes a lightning rod, the electricity goes right to the ground without danger. When flashbacks occur for a patient who is grounded, the energy passes through safely. Without being grounded, lightning will destroy whatever it touches in its attempt to get to the ground. If the patient is not grounded, flashbacks wreak havoc.

With Victoria, I attempted to use grounding to create physical sensations that would draw her back to the present moment. I encouraged her to try physical exertion, such as running in place or doing push-ups that would increase her heart rate. Exercising in this way enabled her, through her body, to focus on the "now." It is a way to reclaim control over the body from the autonomic nervous system response arising from flashbacks. This physical approach to re-taking control is often far more effective than words. Physical activity was the key to help Victoria gain control over her thoughts.

Progress toward Self-Healing

I felt optimistic that Victoria would do her homework faithfully, and I was not disappointed. Victoria's work away from my office paid off. She drove the 920 km in her beat-up truck to see me about ten times during the first year of therapy, then eight times in the second year. She also continued to see the social worker therapist near her home for a year, until that therapist moved away and their sessions ended.

During the following few years, Victoria saw me in sessions that were more and more widely spaced apart until we had only one or two sessions a year. As noted, she saw me for about 50 hours, roughly two hours per session, over a span of seven years. Victoria had been molested for many years. She had been in and out of hospitals with multiple treatment protocols attempted by numerous psychiatrists. Analyzing this in terms of time or economic investment, the mere 50 hours of psychotherapy, with no hospitalizations during those years, was an incredibly short and cost-effective process.

Initially, therapy was intensive, as Victoria's multiplicity system contained highly emotional elements that were in conflict. I worked individually with some very vivid and highly emotional alters. Later, I learned that there were a few more members in the system of which I was originally unaware. Eventually, I took on a supervisory role because the "inner therapist" among the alters began to take over. Victoria conducted active self-directed therapy at home, and even set up video recordings of her therapy sessions with the alters.

This self-directed therapy turned the dynamics of dissociation to creative and productive use as the "inner therapist" provided therapy for the traumatized alters. While Victoria felt the need to send me copies of these recorded sessions, the content was not critical to the therapy I conducted with her in our office sessions. The alters were cooperating with each other, and therefore were not my focus. The fact that the self-directed therapy was of benefit is the important point. The office sessions were used to continue to guide and supervise her self-directed work, focusing on the process rather than the content.

Victoria was able to return to work within months, deciding to avoid working with abuse survivors. Although therapy continued to help her improve, she still was visited by anxiety and depression. Given her life-long history of depression, I believed the temporary use of an anti-depressant was justified so I put her back on one. As she had spent years on antidepressants without improvement prior to psychotherapy, I am confident that psychotherapy was the reason for her healing. This pharmaceutical treatment was used solely as an adjunct to psychotherapy.

Controlling Flashbacks Through Ritual

In order to recall and process her childhood trauma, Victoria had started to make sketches of the events from her childhood. Taking my cue from her, I devised a method whereby she could safely revisit the traumatic scenes at will through her drawings and writings. She designated a special book for this purpose. The critical step was to learn when and how to stop.

Whenever Victoria's emotions became too intense, she was instructed to ceremoniously close the book, put it in its special drawer, and go out for a walk. Ritualizing this cycle of activity became an act of empowerment.

The assumption of control over memories reverses the usual pattern in PTSD, where a victim is subject to repeated flooding of unwelcome intrusive memories. Learning to control the flashbacks that had seemed uncontrollable instilled a confidence in Victoria that the therapy was progressing effectively.

Ongoing Mentorship

As a trained counselor herself, Victoria knew what she needed to do in therapy. My job was simply to maintain contact with her and help her alters to work cooperatively. In later years, some of the alters who felt very comfortable with me frequently jumped out to talk to me. They would appear very briefly, as if only to be acknowledged. They had a habit of appearing without warning during the sessions in my office, and never at my invitation.

It was quite unnerving when they appeared, so suddenly and so real. This was especially true with the "horny one." She would appear, speaking in a low pitched, hoarse, throaty voice, raw with sexual cravings. It was unclear as to whether or not this alter regarded me as a sexual object. My approach, as with all the alters, was to simply maintain the boundaries as psychotherapeutic witness. This allowed the "horny one" to see that I was not a sexual object for her and, at the same time, it confirmed to the system that I was there solely to help her process her trauma.

When I spoke calmly to the angry alter who was always at odds with the others, she was receptive and listened to what I had to say. Eventually, this alter even began to speak to the horny one on behalf of the other alters, negotiating peace among them. Once change was initiated, the alters improved with apparent ease.

Toward the end of our time together, during our face-to-face visits, I spent most of the time with the "inner therapist" alter. She continued to speak to me like a colleague, respectful of my expertise and following my suggestions. I suspect that by then there was a merging of Victoria and the inner therapist. Our relationship became like a mentorship, with me supervising her therapeutic work, and her seeing me every few months to give a progress report on her "patients." She was no longer the labile, chaotic, severely disabled person whom her doctor had described as psychotic.

The Inner Therapist Takes Over

Therapy with Victoria was terminated after seven years. We did not attempt to do any formal integration. There was no need to pursue that as the intense pathological passions of many of the alters had disappeared. Victoria was no longer bothered by flashbacks. She had returned to, and been engaged in, full time employment for years.

Therapeutic Keys

Each DID patient brings with them different strengths and challenges. The therapist's job is, in part, to help the patient discover and tap into the resources that are already there. Victoria, a trained counselor, was easy to work with. She was committed to her own healing process and had the experience of working with the trauma of other abuse survivors.

Even those patients who have no such background can learn to improvise and offer support to the victim alters under treatment if they are willing to do the work. Having the system assign one alter to be "co-therapist" or "comforter" has the advantage of encouraging self-therapy as homework.

The therapist's job is to set the stage for self-healing. The aim of the therapist is to make his/her job obsolete.

Chapter 8 Carla - External Obstacles to Healing

Social and domestic environments can have a powerful influence on the outcome of therapy. They can be so powerful as to completely undermine what a therapist can do. Carla had been waiting years for her disorder to be correctly diagnosed. Even after her DID was recognized, it was not possible to find a therapist to help her within hundreds of kilometers of her home town.

Carla did not have the stamina or resourcefulness of Victoria. She was dependent on her husband, who was rapidly losing his patience. He resented having to come all the way to Vancouver just to have monthly therapy sessions or even coming to sessions that were several months apart. This case underscores the obstacles to healing that can arise despite strong motivation on the part of both the patient and the psychiatrist.

Carla was a 45 year old nurse. She presented with a typical description of DID. She had been seen by six psychiatrists and one psychologist since her first contact with mental health professionals in her mid-twenties. Some of their reports were in her medical records. There had been six admissions to hospitals for depression during the past 13 years.

She came to see me from a city near the border of Alberta, accompanied by her fourth husband. They had been married at that point for six years. Carla had a long history of being abused, first by her birth mother and stepmother, then by her previous husbands. She also had a history of alcohol abuse. Three hours were allotted for her assessment interview.

Her general practitioner sent along consultation reports by the two psychiatrists who had seen her during the previous three years. Since she was living in a remote area of the province, her treatment and ongoing care was given by visiting psychiatrists who flew in every fortnight from Vancouver.

The reports I received were thorough. The diagnoses listed were depression, bipolar disorder, fibromyalgia, chronic fatigue syndrome, and borderline personality disorder. Each psychiatrist had mentioned in their report that Carla had "some dissociative features." However, in their discussion of the diagnosis and patient management, dissociation was never mentioned again. Emphasis was made on the mood disorder aspect of her symptoms, and an anti-convulsant had been added to her medications as a mood stabilizer.

At one time, Carla was on three different antidepressants concurrently, indicating the concentrated effort of the visiting psychiatrists to treat her depression. MMPI (Minnesota Multiphasic Personality Inventory), an elaborate psychological test, was administered by a psychologist. This test missed the dissociative aspect of the clinical picture.

Once the diagnosis is established as depression, whether it is bipolar, major depressive disorder or dysthymia, treatment will be generally narrowed down to the choice of medications. Treatment options are seen as limited to the type of drug, the dosage, and potential combinations. This had been the case of Carla's treatment for years.

Carla's Symptoms

Carla came straight to the point. Her chief complaint was having discreet voices in her head. These were the voices of about 20 females, two males and a few children. As noted before, the voices of different alters in DID patients do not have the flavor of schizophrenic hallucinations. By asking the patient for more details concerning these "voices," one can distinguish schizophrenia from DID.

Carla offered to show me her diary. It was filled with entries in different handwritings as though from different people. This is also characteristic of DID patients.

I had never before had a patient come prepared to show me her diary in the assessment interview. Access to a patient's handwriting in her diary is one of the most useful and illuminating diagnostic aids for DID, leading me to believe that this patient was eager to help me make the correct diagnosis.

There was solid evidence of DID on the pages of her diary. The entries consisted of chaotic and contradictory points of view, with parts erased. Sometimes they were in adult handwritings and sometimes in children's handwritings. With a proper index of suspicion, one could see they were entries from different alters. Carla also complained that when she tried to write in her diary, she would keep tearing up the pages as soon as she had written something. These are all indicators of a likely DID.

There were numerous episodes of time-loss. According to her husband, it occurred on a daily basis. Time-loss may be considered to be a cardinal symptom of DID, and this alone should have almost clinched the diagnosis.

There were many things she had acquired that were out of character with her tastes and preferences. Being a rather modest person, she was shocked to find some highly provocative sexy dresses in her shopping bag, which she obviously had bought. These outfits were presumably purchased by one or more sexually preoccupied or acting out alters.

She took great pains in making shopping decisions, and her husband often had to help in her grocery shopping. This is also common in DID, likely due to having to deal with the concurrently conflicting opinions of many alters.

Since her teens, Carla had engaged in numerous episodes of self-inflicted injury. This had ceased since she met her current husband. Self-inflicted injury is often due to one alter acting hatefully toward another. Usually, it is one accusing the other of cowardly and passive behavior, of weakly succumbing to the assaults of the abuser. However, this conduct is also commonly found in borderline personality disorder patients. This is another reason for DID patients sometimes being misdiagnosed as having BPD.

Carla was highly efficient and could multi-task easily. Multi-tasking is easy when a bipolar patient is in the hypomanic phase. However, it is an ongoing feature of DID rather than a cyclical one.

Outcome

The outcome of this case was sad. Carla was living hundreds of kilometers away, and she likely would have required fairly long term psychotherapy. I tried to arrange for treatment in her hometown and contacted the local mental health personnel. Unfortunately, the social worker/therapist living there was uncomfortable with DID, and felt too inexperienced to deal with Carla. She was unwilling to take up the challenge to learn to do therapy with a DID patient. The visiting psychiatrist for that region did not support any such therapeutic effort based on his skepticism of DID as a genuine psychiatric disorder. Further, Carla's husband was losing patience with the domestic turmoil. Instead of finding the diagnosis a relief, a helpful context in which to understand his wife, he saw it as an excuse for her not to get better. "I have put up with the crap for too long," he said. As a result, Carla was under great pressure to get better quickly.

In sending her to me, the referring mental health professionals had hoped that I could suggest either a better medication or a better medication cocktail. They did not find it helpful to bring up a new, unfamiliar diagnosis which would have required a complete paradigm shift for them. In short, everyone was looking for a quick pharmaceutical fix. It was as if Carla had been sick for too long, and no one had any patience left for her.

It is not uncommon to have difficulty finding a therapist to treat DID patients. Even in a major city like Vancouver, it was quite hard for individuals suffering from DID to find one. The situation in outlying regions of the province is worse. Mental Health Services is forced to rely on visiting psychiatrists whose primary role is simply to assess new patients and adjust medication periodically for long term cases.

While such periodic visits might suffice if the task was solely to assess patients on long term medication or write a consultation report, to supervise or actually engage in psychotherapy is another matter entirely. This is especially true when the visiting psychiatrist has no experience treating DID patients. It is even worse when the psychiatrist neither believes the diagnosis nor even in the existence of the disorder. As a result, treatment for Carla was doomed to failure. The local treatment team never came to terms with the diagnosis. Carla returned to see me a few more times, and then I lost contact with her.

I last saw Carla many years ago. I sensed that her husband had reached the end of his patience. There was only one direction her path would take. She would become more disabled, more depressed, and continue to deteriorate. Given the lack of treatment options she would likely continue to encounter, she was at risk of becoming a chronic patient on ever-changing pharmaceutical cocktails. At best, a patient like this ends up in a boarding home. At worst, such a patient finally succeeds at suicide.

A patient like Carla does not spontaneously get better. She presented with all the features that pointed to good outcome; a stable home base, previously high functioning, with relatively low resistance to treatment among the alters. While I was willing to supervise her care by a local therapist from a distance, this offer was rejected. Had a willing therapist been prepared to give proper treatment, Carla might have reclaimed the life she had been denied by her abusers. The absence of support from her spouse and the local mental health system undermined the positive potential in treatment.

The system for the delivery of psychiatric care failed Carla. She is one of the reasons I have written this book. I hope that the result will be that others like Carla will have a better chance to find the right help.

Therapeutic Keys

External support is critical for healing. The prognosis for DID patients that lack external support is simply not good.

DID therapy is not unreasonably complicated, particularly when a patient has motivation to heal and is not resisting DID treatment. Even a therapist with no experience treating DID can be effectively mentored to help a patient.

Chapter 9 Doris - Non-Directive Therapy

Doris had been severely traumatized by incest. She initially presented as a stable, somewhat normal individual, with a strong undercurrent of major disturbance. For Doris, the approach was "non-directive" therapy. With other patients, it was necessary to ask questions, make suggestions, or re-direct. With Doris, therapy was close to the Taoist principle of wu wei[30], sometimes understood as a creative quietude or action through non-action. This is the opposite of passively zoning out. It is a place of total attention in the present that has no element of strain.

This approach to therapy requires the complete attention and effort on the part of both the patient and the therapist. To an observer, it might seem that nothing of significance was happening. Therapeutic sessions all appeared like casual social encounters. It could even be seen as boring or overly simplistic. However, the proof is in the pudding: Doris's recovery was tremendous and inspiring.

Doris looked and behaved in a low key way, hiding her inner turmoil well. However, from the very beginning, she knew what she wanted, where she needed to go, and the pace that she needed to follow. As I aligned myself with

---

[30]Common translation of *wu wei* is non-action or effortless action, which falls hand in hand, in "naturalness". It is seen in the metaphors of flowing water that cuts through rocks and the natural beauty of un-carved wood. The universe works harmoniously in the natural ways. When one applies too much effort, going against nature, one disrupts the natural harmony. Taoism cautions against potentially harmful interference so that goals can be achieved effortlessly. To attain naturalness, one has to identify with the Tao, appreciating simplicity and freeing oneself from self-preoccupation.

her tempo, and listened as genuinely as possible, there was hardly any need to intervene, steer, or direct. We were not rushing to a finish line, nor following an externally defined agenda. Following her lead, therapy was successful.

Doris knew that she needed time to tell, at her own pace, the story of the terrible abuse she had endured with her father. She also needed a caring, respectful parental figure who absolutely would not betray or abuse her. Being listened to in this way, coupled with being given the time she needed to process the trauma, led to her healing.

As she needed to release pent up tensions she had been carrying for decades, many sessions were spent on spontaneously abreacting her childhood abuse. When the material is so heavy, a therapist should not be surprised for the process to be quite repetitive and to take an extended period of time. Doris repeated the same stories dozens of time.

This repetition was obviously necessary for Doris's healing process. Repetition that is not re-traumatization indicates that patients need to tell and re-tell their experience. It is not for the therapist to decide whether the experience has been expressed a sufficient number of times. The therapist must make clear that they are willing to listen and witness so long as the system deems it necessary.

The diagnosis of DID was unambiguous. As with other DID patients, I spent time reassuring the protective alters that no one would be threatened or hurt by the therapy. Some sessions were spent acknowledging the re-organization of her multiplicity system. In this case, re-organizing the multiplicity meant that when certain alters withdrew their willingness to perform a particular function, others were assigned. In effect, this was a re-shuffling of her internal executive cabinet. In addition, Doris needed help negotiating a new relationship with her abusive parents.

Because her therapy followed such an organic course, I have included brief descriptions and details from actual sessions. This is done in order to convey a sense of the therapeutic thread from beginning to end over the course of the nine years. It is noteworthy that there was a total of only 58 hours in actual therapy time.

The session-by-session approach allows one to see how Doris's course of recovery was, like life itself, not a straight progression. It followed a sometimes winding course that took her where she needed to go. It proceeded at a rhythm slow enough to allow for safe and gentle debriefing of traumatic material. It was as if she had been waiting for years for the right circumstances to coalesce so that she could gradually free herself from the burdens of the past.

Session 1

When Doris first saw me, she presented as a high functioning, soft spoken, and poised 32 year old with a strong motivation to get well. She had an engineering degree and was working for a large private company. Calmly, she offered a concise relevant history, giving me exactly the information I would have asked for.

Despite a long history of incest, multiple sexual abuse events, chronic alcohol abuse and chaotic relationships with men, Doris had gone through university and obtained a responsible job. She had been living with a boyfriend for a year.

Before coming to me, she'd seen two therapists. The first was a female psychiatrist who tried to help her with her complaint of sexual difficulties. Although she saw this therapist for more than five years, it was to no avail. During that time, she was living in an alcoholic haze and was completely amnesic about her past sexual abuse. It was unlikely that the treatment ever touched core issues, since the heavy drinking further walled off her memories of childhood abuse. After she was prescribed Ativan, an anxiety medication, she became addicted to it. She had been relying on it ever since.

Doris saw her second therapist for two years. This therapy ended when the therapist, a woman, betrayed her by seducing Doris's boyfriend. I had no way to verify this, but judging from what I came to learn about her in the subsequent years, I have no reason to doubt her.

After years of drinking, Doris had joined AA. She had been clean and sober for five years by the time we met. She had come to see me because intrusive memories of her father's assaults were troubling her at night. She could not remember how old she was when her father's incestuous advances began. She also started remembering other abuses, such as being raped by a babysitter at age four.

These flashbacks had induced a silent rage inside her, expressed as violent dreams. She described how, at times, she felt as though her body was moving independently of her. She also experienced periods during which there was a loss of concentration. Her facade of calm and tranquility appeared to be covering a smoldering volcano of anger threatening to erupt. I reminded myself not to be fooled by her outward calm demeanor.

I did not interrupt her narrative to interrogate her

further about these experiences. Allowing a natural flow of narrative from a patient further fosters trust and safety, necessities for the creation of a therapeutic alliance.

Doris was clear and resolute when she spoke: "I want a therapist and a safe place to talk about what happened." Her determination made me optimistic that she would do well in therapy. Maybe it was the right time in her life for her to confront these haunting memories from the past. The diagnosis initially pointed to severe PTSD with dissociative features, with a high index suspicion for DID.

I left decisions about the frequency and spacing of our sessions entirely to her. After the first session, I saw her two or three times each month for the first year, once or twice each month the second year, and then at intervals spaced out longer over the next seven years.

Session 2

Doris was experiencing much intrusive memory. While she had difficulty describing the abuse in words, she had vivid physical sensations associated with it. She complained of vaginal pain and difficulty using tampons during her period. For years, she'd had recurrent bladder infections and difficulty holding her water. I suspect the early sexual and physical abuse might have caused hyper-sensitization to her urinary tract.

She seemed to brighten a bit as she talked about her dedication to working out in the gym, studying the piano, and oil painting. She was an active member of her church and I took it as a good sign that she felt connected with a community from which she could draw spiritual sustenance. She emphasized that she wanted "spiritual healing" and, possibly because of the work she had done in AA, referred to a higher power that could help her.[31]

Although I knew that Doris was having intrusive flashbacks, she seemed externally calm. To help her manage her internal anxiety, I suggested some conscious breathing exercises, which can be very calming for the nervous system.

It is empowering to realize that something as automatic and unconscious as breathing can be modulated and controlled. Someone who has learned to slow down, direct, and move their breath may come to appreciate that they can also slow down, direct, and interrupt flashbacks, along with the accompanying overwhelming emotions. It is a simple thing, but so long as we are alive, the breath is always with us. Establishing it as a refuge[32] has extraordinary benefits in therapy.

Session 3

We continued to talk about establishing a safe place. Before venturing into any of her trauma history, I wanted Doris to develop the internal resources necessary to enable her to put herself in a safe place. In addition, we needed to

---

[31] Almost all my patients who did well in therapy had a spiritual connection, irrespective if they were practicing Christians or engaging in Buddhist meditation. Marsha Linehan, a therapist and researcher who also suffered from borderline personality disorder, recalls the religious experience that transformed her as a young woman. Her work with BPD patients and mindfulness, applicable to sexual abuse survivors, deserves more attention and clinical application.

[32] This has been discussed in the chapter on Victoria (Chapter 7) and Laura (Chapter 10), but is repeated here to underscore its importance.

continue to build our relationship so that she felt safe in the environment and secure in the knowledge that I would not abandon or exploit her.

Retrieving trauma memory is not difficult, but the point is dealing with what happens afterwards. Like a diver who surfaces too quickly and gets the bends (decompression sickness), memories that come to the surface too fast, without preparation or follow up, can be dangerous. If too much intense trauma material comes up too fast, and there is no safe anchorage, a person may become re-traumatized.

Doris knew that she was not ready to plunge into talking about the traumatic past. She paid full attention to our discussion of building a safe place and using the breath. She was likely continuing to assess me in order to decide when she could tell me more about herself.

Session 4

Doris started telling me that she had always had a boyfriend, but immediately "lost" herself when she had sex. She meant that as soon as sexual contact began, she dissociated. Then, she told me about time-loss. The longest time-loss was several hours, and was usually related to sex. I suspected that during sexual contact, an alter had taken over so that she experienced it as time-loss. At that point, I did not deem it necessary to tell her my DID suspicion.

Once she spoke of time-loss, she opened up and gave me an entire list of DID symptoms. This included items at home found in the wrong drawers, articles she had bought with "stupid orange color" etc. Then she talked about her inner reality. She identified the following alters:

1. A Doris who went to work

2. A different Doris who went to AA meetings

3. The little girl that had the bladder problems

4. The self-destructive one

5. "Ice lady" who picked up men

It was during Session 4 that she spontaneously revealed her multiplicity. I did not ask any leading question pertaining to DID, but the session confirmed my earlier suspicions. Again, I did not tell her my diagnostic opinion. My lack of judgmental reaction to all she had told me must have reassured her that I understood her condition. I decided that she could come to her own diagnostic conclusion when it was appropriate for her to do so.

Session 5

By doing her breathing exercises and bringing her attention to the body, especially her bladder, she started remembering the bladder pain associated with her father's sadistic abuse. She spent the whole session relating this sexual abuse history. I did not ask questions or prompt her in any way, but listened with my full attention to what she needed to explore.

The therapeutic container of the office is a private sanctuary, where patients who feel impelled to talk can be received and deeply listened to by someone who has no personal agenda. When hearing about trauma, therapists would do well to provide that place where patients understand that they are neither being judged nor probed. For Doris, the timing was right to reveal her traumatic memory to an empathic witness.

There is no need here to detail the deviant nature and intensity of the abuse, both physical and sexual. What was striking was that her telling me about the abuse was not triggering flashbacks. Doris could feel her bodily reaction without being swept away by uncontrolled emotions, dissociation and resultant re-traumatization. That is the essence of healing traumatic wounds.

Through safely sharing the story of what happened, Doris learned to uncouple her traumatic memories of abuse from the physiological turmoil of her flashbacks. When the person is ready and the situation is right, therapy can enable that critical skill of transforming implicit memory into explicit memory. Doris was able to change the memories' intense, almost electric, charge into explicit autobiographical memories which then gradually lost their power.

We talked about empowerment. While she was prepared to go after her father in court, I kept a reserved silence. I was not in favor of seeking legal remedies for sexually abusive violations that happened so long ago. There is a very specific reason for this: The public challenges to their accusations are difficult for most survivors of abuse to tolerate. In addition, it is very difficult to win a case based primarily on the evidence of decades-old personal recollection. Losing the case could have potentially dangerous consequences for the patient.

The only time it may be justified to pursue an abuser in court is if the abuser is continuing to abuse the patient, or is likely abusing others.

Session 6

In this session, Doris brought in a two page letter that she silently handed to me. It contained this message: "I have watched and seen many things over the years. Many people have come and gone. People who said they were here to help but they were not. Each had their own motives and their own plans....they have been doctors, church ministers, teachers, counselors, friends.....None could face the truth and so they pushed her back into her own darkness. All the time I have watched. I am still here listening. There will be no more betrayals, broken promises, no more false hopes. That has been my job....to watch. I cannot let her be hurt any more, and I will not leave her alone. I will always (be) here to listen. What is your interest in her? Is she some specimen.....? I am not to be played with. I am in the end in control. I will take over and protect her........" It was signed "The Watcher." The writing was distinct from her usual handwriting, which I had seen on the intake form she filled out during her initial office visit.

The letter signaled to me that while she was starting to trust me more, a protective alter was alarmed. That alter, fearing her at risk of being hurt, stepped in to issue me a direct warning.

I read the letter aloud with her. I thanked the alter who issued the stern warning for looking after the security of the system all these years, and for acting as a protector. I asked her or him, as I did not know the gender, to continue this important work. We talked about trust. Partly because of her experiences of betrayal from her former therapist and others, she feared being hurt yet again in therapy.

Having acknowledged and thanked that alter, I kept my communication to her at a minimum. If there was a need to tell me more, she could easily write another letter or simply pop out to speak to me. This approach significantly limits unnecessary probing into the individual histories of each alter.

Session 7

Doris told me of more dissociative symptoms. She found out she had two distinct handwritings at work. Further, she sometimes suddenly felt disoriented at work, forgetting how to perform routine tasks.

Once she felt reassured, she had much to process. The unloading of her story in a place and time of her own choosing was highly therapeutic.

Session 8

She came to her own conclusion that she was DID.

"Someone took over and I was out the whole evening."

"Anything to do with sex, I am out."

"In my drawer I have garter belts, fish-net stockings, black negligee and black high heels."

"Sometimes I've had a blackout, and woken up in a closet."

She confessed that she experienced many moments when she felt a loss of control and could not resist certain urges, even though they were clearly unwise impulses to follow. For example, she might approach a stranger, black out, and wake up later in a hotel finding that she had spent the night with him.

The session marked the beginning of true insight and breaking down of amnestic barriers. Doris was starting to observe her own pathology objectively. Since she was progressing so well under her own steam, I held back any active direction during the session. Nevertheless, she was aware that she had my undivided attention and genuine support.

A new alter came out during this session, a cynic who did not want to talk with me. She simply wanted to let me know of her presence. No doubt her surfacing was another warning to me. I acknowledged her and let her be.

Therapeutic progress includes treading on dangerous ground. The consequence for protective alters is that they feel uneasy. I knew that the cynical alter as well as the protective alter would likely be stirring agitation inside Doris, but the manifestation of this alter signaled an increasing therapeutic alliance with the whole system.

Session 9

She told me that in her daily journal she frequently had written letters to herself in different handwritings. I took the opportunity to encourage such communications. I reassured them all that every one of them was important for the whole system. I also reassured them that therapy was not a threat to their existence. I explained that no one would be eliminated. I further emphasized, given her church connection, that exorcism had no place in DID therapy.

Doris was continuing to have difficulties handling her parents. As we discussed ways to deal with them, I took a much more active role.

Session 10

She talked about not pursuing her father in court. I had underscored the danger of re-traumatization in court as well as the likely futility of trying to prove unwitnessed sexual intercourse from decades ago. She agreed there would be a risk of more loss than gain through seeking legal redress.

She told me that she had decided to stop picking up strangers. She felt strong enough to stay out of sexual relationships for the time being. It was her new resolution. Her progress in these ten sessions was remarkable.

Session 11

She told me that there was some re-organization of the inner family, with the director resigning. Like an observer, witnessing but not participating, I sat silently through the meeting of the alters. I was both privileged and pleased to watch the therapeutic process unfold in this way.

Session 12

A new alter called Martha, the "inner helper,"

showed up. This care-taking role appeared to be a new role assigned to an existing alter.

Doris was having some inner struggles because of the decision to have no more casual sexual encounters.

Session 13

We talked about how living with multiplicity is like living in a dormitory with many comings and goings, and voices chatting all the time. However, she was handling them well. She was able to continue carrying out her duties at work despite the reshuffling and turmoil of her inner world.

At night, she would brush her teeth three or four times, because different alters insisted on brushing in their individual ways. It was clear that a few of the alters were still insisting on their individuality.

We talked about Christmas, which was coming soon. For many patients with early trauma, Christmas is a particularly stressful time. It is a time that may trigger bad memories while simultaneously exerting tremendous social pressure. People may have to face toxic family members and other relatives, to struggle with being able to say no and set boundaries, or to maintain the pretense of being joyful. Doris gave me hope that she would be able to protect herself at this time when she said simply, "You have taught me to honor my parts".

Session 14

Her daily life was calming down, and her concentration had improved at work. She was continuing to attend the 12 step program in AA.

While she was still aware of some parts expressing anger toward me as the therapist for causing changes in the system, she made a number of heartening comments. These included; "I feel I can recover," "I have the right to have a safe place," and "I have the right to have space." It seemed that the many alters were coming together. They were being more cooperative and working as a team.

Session 15

As soon as Doris came in, she said she wanted to appraise her own therapeutic progress after seven months of twice-a-month sessions. As she looked back on the typically high-stress time of a family Christmas, she realized that she had negotiated it well, and congratulated herself. I was pleased to see that she was learning to affirm and encourage herself.

In her inner family, there remained some turmoil. There were alters shifting roles as well as several alters receding within the system. This kind of political shake up is not unusual in DID patients. I was gratified that she was so aware of what was going on inside, and able to talk about it with equanimity. She mentioned some other positives: Her shopping compulsion had disappeared and rather than following the temptation to replace it with a new compulsion, she had taken time instead to work on a new skill, Tae Kwan Do. She felt happy with her progress and was looking forward to the next six months.

I was surprised to hear her mention rather casually that she had married her boyfriend in a civil ceremony. She had not brought up the wedding before, no doubt because it was not part of her therapeutic agenda. Having such a clear idea of one's therapeutic goals is unusual, but Doris knew exactly what she wanted from me. There was no doubt that she was capable of processing any thoughts she had about marriage within herself, with friends, or even with the boyfriend himself.

Doris's ability to so clearly engage in her own therapeutic agenda is rare. However, the therapist needs to remain vigilant of the serious pitfalls that can adversely impact such a self-directed patient. The principal risk is that she could become so fixated on her own agenda that she would not be able to respond to unexpected twists and turns that might arise in her life. Fortunately, Doris was flexible enough that she did not develop this kind of tunnel vision. However, her abilities and flexibility does not mean that the therapist can relax their own vigilance and become lazy.

Session 16

Doris arrived in my office looking rather flushed. At once, she spilled out her worries that she could not handle the "sick people" around her. Referring to her relatives, she stated to me in a level-headed tone, "I need your support to say no to these people."

It is hard to break the habit of letting toxic people invade one's boundaries. I encouraged her warmly, and gave her what she had asked for – my unconditional support. Since Doris had been struggling with the ways that people were trying to take over her life since she was a child, I was careful not to take the reins from her, but to simply do what she asked of me. Refraining from directing her was an expression of support, of confidence in her basic intelligence, and of her ability to heal.

Session 17

I got another letter, in yet another distinct handwriting, from a newly identified alter expressing fear of what was going to happen to her (the alter). It was a long letter telling me of her insecurity, the fear that her defenses were being broken down by me, her fear of being shut out, of being rendered useless, abandoned and eliminated. This letter seemed a natural response to the changes that were happening. It confirmed for me that therapy was progressing well.

I took this opportunity to address this alter directly. I reiterated my belief, as if in a classroom and knowing that all the other alters were listening, that each alter was important. I stated again that I did not want to eliminate anyone. Because all the alters were inhabiting the same body, I again urged better communication, cooperation, and coordination to help them live a better life.

Doris had been able to keep her resolution not to pick up men at AA. Our session digressed into talking about her hobbies and pastimes. She talked about music and we discussed our favorite composers. She was also a voracious reader. While a more casual, friendly chat about outside interests may seem irrelevant to therapy, it often helps to forge deeper bonding that enhances the therapeutic alliance. As in any psychotherapy, but especially with a

DID patient, such bonding is a decisive factor contributing to a successful outcome.

Session 18

Doris spontaneously brought up an episode of her father's abuse in a calm and composed manner. I was taken aback by the level of detail she shared. As I was affirmatively not looking for details, it is clear that she had determined that presenting this level of information was necessary for her healing. This kind of calm and peaceful recollection with the therapist's acknowledgment is a deep healing experience.

The angry alter continued to pose problems and resist change. However, inviting this alter out to speak with me had an immediate calming effect. She became much mellower afterwards. It was astonishing how positively responded to engagement with me. This was one of the few times that I engaged so actively in therapy with this patient.

Doris told me that writing journals and painting really helped the system.

It is noteworthy that this 18th session was the first time Doris presented anything beyond a generic description of abuse. This is another reminder to therapists that actively holding still, neither ignoring nor demanding details, is most important. It must be clear that one is fully present to witness when such things are brought up. However, one must allow the patient to bring such things forward at the time of her choosing. This furthers the empowerment so necessary to healing.

Session 19

Without my instigation, Doris reported that she had started "round-table conferences" at home with the inner family of alters. The result was that the whole system became quieter and calmer, allowing her to sleep better. She was able now to remember most of her childhood. This included not only the traumatic experiences with her father, but also ordinary events. As much as DID patients may need to get past the denial and amnestic barriers associated with early trauma, the ability to remember good times from childhood as well signifies profound improvement.

Session 20

Doris told me she just read a book on MPD. I realized where the idea of a "round-table conference" had come from. It is likely where she picked up a lot of healing suggestions.

Session 21

We talked about handling sick relationships again. She also remembered more abuse experiences.

Session 22

Even though I was of a different ethnicity and demeanor than her father, it is not surprising that the intensity of the relationship she had been developing with me, an adult male, would trigger the feelings of rage that she had toward her father. This session was spent in having one alter come out telling me how she hated me, and how she felt about me taking away her power. She resented the way I represented authority. She told me that I was threatening her security, ambition and personal desires.

I understood that this alter was distressed by the changes wrought by therapy. All she needed was some reassurance from me that I respected her, that she was important in the system, and that I had no intention of taking away her power. I told her that I understood that it was hard to give up some sense of separateness. She had come to realize the necessity of this as she realized that she was sharing the same body as all the others.

Being able to express anger in a session can show a patient that she sees her relationship with the therapist as strong enough to tolerate honest emotions, including rage. The non-defensive response of the therapist enables a corrective emotional experience.

Session 23

Doris told me that the "Ice lady" had just joined the team.

During the session, a "little one" wanted to speak to me. It was heart-warming to meet this eight year old child and listen to her story. She told me her pet name Chèrie. She told me about the house in the country, about going to school, and about her love for the fish and ducks in the pond. But, she did not like the barn. It was scary. I spent almost a half-hour with this child alter, who came out to seek affirmation and approval. I responded as a warm, comforting, appropriately paternal figure.

Afterwards Doris had a severe headache, a common complaint associated with switching alters for many DID patients.

Session 24

Doris explained to me the significance of my seeing the "little one." Apparently, she was the leader of a group of child alters. Doris told me that the "little one" needed encouragement and approval. She then went on to talk about the abuse in more detail. Obviously, there was still more trauma to process.

Session 25

As the lengthy abreaction continued, I could sense that the groups of alters inside were paying full attention. This was especially true for the groups of children, each of them carrying specific memories of trauma and abuse. I repeated previous suggestions for keeping in touch with the body, finding a safe place, and learning how to listen to the body.

When I spoke, I could feel the whole system listening and participating in the healing process. I felt I was holding the hands of a group of children in a circle of healing, who were each telling me some of the terrifying experiences they had undergone. They were beginning to understand that they were no longer alone.

I was greatly moved by the courage needed to display that level of vulnerability in this powerful work.

Session 26

We spent much time learning to handle relationships with people; including her husband, friends and relatives. Early interpersonal violations create great difficulty for trauma survivors in discerning boundaries between themselves and others. I had to teach her how to draw the line to defend her own territory, including with the abusive parents with whom she was still socially connected. Doris still had to deal with her abusive father who wanted to pretend that they had a normal father-daughter relationship.

Had Doris expressed the desire to never see her abuser again in any context, I would have been equally supportive and equally non-judgmental. Again, following the patient's insights and needs must always be considered.

Session 27

I got a letter from Doris saying, "Dear sir, Life is better, happier....Thank you." I assumed this came from an alter that found it easier to express gratitude in writing than in speaking.

We talked about piano music and the pleasure of working on some difficult pieces. We discussed how experiencing the joy of making music or capturing light through oil on a canvas, are gratifying experiences. By engaging herself in creative activities, Doris generated feelings of mastery and pleasure. Having been deprived of these by the abuse experiences, she was now able to reclaim those feelings.

Sharing these kinds of interests verbally with a

therapist may allow patients relief from the strain of always being in that role. It is also an opportunity for the patient to experience the pleasure of a safe, friendly and cordial conversation. At the right time, talking about playing Mozart or painting may also help patients appreciate their own strengths and assets beyond the world of therapy.

It is helpful for therapists to know more than just psychotherapy in their work. It enables them to build additional support bridges to the patient, thus strengthening the therapeutic alliance.

Session 28

Doris talked about work, and how she had to struggle to stay on top in a competitive environment. She was the acting head of the department when the boss went on vacation. She suddenly switched and talked about the dissociative group inside. She gave me some names. There were eight principal ones with some "subsidiary" ones. Then, suddenly, she was talking of integration: "We are coming together." She imagined them "joining hands and standing together."

From Session 29 to 33

Sessions were spent on more abreaction about her father's abuse. There were many repetitions, and one might wonder if such repetitions were necessary. With such a prolonged, horrendous history of abuse by the father, this traumatic memory would take considerable time to process and heal. There are no short-cuts to healing for people who have had their trust betrayed so deeply as incest survivors.

I remained confident that if she wanted to repeat herself, it must be necessary for her healing.

She also suddenly announced that she had made the difficult decision to quit a two-pack-a-day smoking habit. I would not have advised her to quit smoking at this time in her therapy. However, as it came from her, I was simply supportive.

It was not surprising that there were marital issues. For DID patients, marriage is very complicated. It is often the case that some alters are likely very fond of the spouse while others are not.

She offered a more detailed description of the ten alters inside. I think she was trying to let me know her more clearly.

She had been doing meditation regularly. I encouraged her to keep it up as well as to write in her daily journal, a practice that was helping her to integrate her new learning.

Then she talked about the group inside being together and "joining hands."

Session 34

It has now been six years since Doris started therapy. She was now coming to see me twice a year. She had just got her "ten year cake" at AA. She was doing regular meditation. She reported that the inner battles were quelled.

She described an experience of going to a

chiropractor that had triggered more memories of abuse. She was able to calm down fairly fast, after which she felt only sadness. We were beginning to think of terminating therapy at this point.

Session 35

For the first time, there was a crisis. Something had happened to open new floodgates of the terrifying past. Someone had sued her father. It was another of his many victims.

A lawyer had called to ask her questions, with the possibility of dragging her into court to testify. Needless to say, such an event would have triggered more memories, without the safety of titrated exposure and a supportive empathic presence. I had always let her decide when and what to say about the abuse at her own pace. The lawyer's questions had agitated her, had triggered not only more memories and anger toward her father, but also rage toward her mother for not protecting her.

The child who does not know what to do with the anger she has built up toward both parents may carry a lifelong weight of rage in the heart. The abuser may be unaware of the hostile energy accumulated in his name. The primary sufferer is still the victim whose heart is darkened by hatred and rage. The wound is healed only when the victim arrives at the point that she is no longer hostage to the abuser; no longer hostage in fact <u>or</u> in memory.

It was clear to me that Doris was not completely healed. Although it had seemed we were nearing the end of therapy, the quiet was a lull before this new storm. It only took a few questions to re-open the wound again.

Next 12 Sessions

More memories were coming back. Doris felt like drinking, going to parties, and beating up her mother. The impulse to pick up men was hard to resist. She described her state of mind as "full of rage and blackness." Ativan, which she had been taking sparingly, no longer worked and she could not sleep. She was taken aback by the intensity of the rage toward her mother. It was indeed a crisis.

Her marriage was also in a state of crisis. She was cold and distant toward her husband, even though she was not consciously angry with him. He could not cope with her rejection.

Doris saw me 12 times over the next eight months. I supported her in her decision to distance herself from toxic relatives, to focus on her mental health, and to continue with her own healing practice. In these sessions I was much more active, contrary to the approach previously described.

As consistent depressive symptoms seemed to have invaded her physically, I started her on a low dose of an anti-depressant and referred her to a colleague for conjoint marital therapy. The medication helped. She reported sleeping better and was no longer waking up in the middle of the night. She began having a sense of hope.

Using pharmaceuticals as an adjunct to the crucible of psychotherapy can be of benefit. This is especially true when they are used selectively rather than as an automatic first recourse. The fact that her sleeping pattern had changed for the worse, and then after medication for the better, confirmed the appropriateness of the pharmaceutical adjunct.

Following a few months of more frequent sessions, Doris began to regain her equilibrium. She started taking courses to prepare for a better job, and began sending out resumes.

She was able to see herself and her actions with the distance conferred by greater mindfulness. She was able to catch herself in that moment between the impulse to act and the decision to act. When she felt attracted to a man, she could check inside. She was able to recognize that following the trajectory of her desire in an impulsive way would lead to disaster. With remarkable insight, she also said that she was now more co-conscious with all the alters, "I am aware when I am turning into a bitch." Developing this level of meta-awareness is difficult for all of us. No doubt her years of practicing meditation and journal writing were helpful for her.

She had learned to be much more in control of her relationships with negative family members. She had also learned to set some boundaries, firmly telling her mother "Please stop calling me," rather than simply hanging up. She complained that she could no longer dissociate and missed that option, as this form of checking out had sometimes served her well. This was interesting, but not too surprising, since she had been so accustomed to dissociating.

Her marital relationship had started to settle down somewhat. However, she and her husband agreed to live apart and simply date each other again. At the same time, she started to seek out more healthy relationships, saying "I want people in my life who have their own life." The healthier she became, the more remote she felt from her husband. She thought that he fulfilled a role in her life, and she in his, when she was in distress. But when she felt better, she found them more and more detached from each other. By the end of the year, she had found a more satisfying job, and also ended her marriage.

The next 11 sessions

In the years that followed, she saw me every six months or so, always at a time of her own choosing. These sessions were like periodic progress check-ins, and I kept my attitude of non-directive receptivity. Eventually, she told me that she no longer hated her father, but just felt sorry for him.

Reflections on Doris's Healing and Recovery

From our first session through our last session eight years and ten months later, Doris had undergone a total of 58 hours of psychotherapy. Given the years of abuse and the severity of damage in her childhood and adult life, her recovery within such a short number of hours in therapy is a testament to the power of bringing together a correct diagnosis, a motivated patient and appropriate psychotherapy.

This young woman had experienced some of the worst traumas I have come across. The most important persons in her early life, an incestuous and perverted violent father along with an alternately carping and neglectful mother, had inflicted great damage upon her.

Throughout her adult life, people tried to cheat and take advantage of her. Even when she came to me, she still had to deal with both parents insisting on maintaining the illusion of normal parent-daughter relationships. She had gone through a long, tortuous course seeking a therapist able to identify and treat her disorder.

The process of DID therapy is like bearing witness to a crime that was committed decades ago. Finding a therapist she could trust, and to whom she could tell her story in a safe place, was the gateway to resolution and healing. I let the system decide when and what to do during therapy sessions, giving the alters the attention, empowerment, acknowledgment and respect that they needed. That was the essence of her psychotherapy.

Although the alters carried intense emotions, my communications with them did not lead to theatrics in my office. The letters she brought in offered opportunities to speak directly to the alters and responding to each of their concerns in a matter of fact way, acknowledging their place in the system, the memories they held, and the fears that constricted them.

The letters, again, were a golden opportunity to thank the alters for their communications, to thank them for the roles they played in preserving the system through extremely dark times, and to remind them of the need to cooperate among themselves. It did not take much time to talk to any of the alters. The longest, about a half hour, was spent with the "little one." Most of our sessions were very quiet. I did not spend time psychoanalyzing each alter as there was no such need presented.

At the end of therapy, the troublesome alters seemed to have quietly receded into the background. Crises will arise in the future, and under stress the alters will no doubt come to the fore again, but perhaps with their strengths positively applied. This was the case with the chiropractic incident. With Doris's improved self-awareness and resilience, she had a much greater repertoire of strategies for coping with stress. These had been insufficient at the time of the call from the lawyer, but were much stronger at this later point.

It was rewarding as well as a great pleasure to watch Doris's growth. Through the support of appropriately applied psychotherapy and the judicious use of medication as an adjunct, Doris was able to do the necessary work.

In looking at this through a cost/benefit analysis, over the course of almost nine years, the medical insurance agency paid for 58 hours of psycho-therapy. There were no other psychiatric expenses – hospital or otherwise beyond the brief period of medication used as an adjunct to treatment.

Epilogue

Twelve months after the last session, Doris asked for an appointment to report on her current life situation. This was the last time I saw her. In her soft and calm voice, she told me the following:

> She was still working for the same company in a job she liked.
> She now owned a condo.
> She had been celibate for two years.
> She had some close friends but no boyfriend.

She remembered the past quite clearly but felt OK.

Her parting words:

> Inside it is all quiet.
> No more voices,
> No more raging in my head.
> I can accept people, men and women, and say, 'I love you.'
> I have a strong sense of who I am.
> I can calm down quickly through meditation.

Therapeutic Keys

When alters communicate directly to the therapist, by speaking, writing, painting or otherwise, the therapist must not neglect such golden opportunities. Acknowledge their roles in holding the trauma, in protecting the system during and after the trauma, and in processing it.

This case is an example of a patient who did indeed continue to have a relationship with her abusers, in this case her abusive parents. Nevertheless, she was able to process the trauma and establish the boundaries necessary to heal.

Chapter 10 - Limited Successes and Failures

Prolonged and severe trauma that occurs before the body and personality have developed enough to withstand a violation of trust and assault devastates the psyche. People whose sense of basic trust has been violated early and repeatedly may be unable to ever let down their guard. Treating such damaged people can be very difficult. As much as it might be tempting to construct a narrative of steady progress and triumph with all my DID patients, I have not done so, as such an account would be misleading.

This chapter offers further examples of work with DID patients where improvement, if present at all, was very limited. There are also examples where the treatment went nowhere because of internal and/or external obstacles to therapeutic healing.

Some DID patients simply could not engage in therapy. Others who tried it showed no improvement at all. Some patients came in only once, and others dropped out after a number of sessions for different reasons. Sometimes therapy did not seem to be taking hold, despite my persistence. One must learn one's therapeutic limits, and clarify the limits of the methods one applies. This can only happen by coming up against those limits.

In Canada, we are fortunate that our Medical Plan of universal coverage allows a psychiatrist to see a patient for so long as necessary. I recognize that the situation where no patient has to be turned away for lack of funds does not apply in many places in the world. The coverage in Canada is critical, but equally critical is having trained therapists that patients can access.

Debbie - Scaling Down Therapeutic Goals

I treated Debbie for five years with sessions two to three weeks apart. She was a woman in her late 50s living a very restricted life. She had a history of memory lapses lasting two months at a time. Through her own detective work, she had figured out that she had been prostituting during those two month lapses.

Debbie's memory of abuse was hazy, almost dream-like. It included rituals as well as a stranger being killed by her father, who was her abuser. I did not seek to determine whether or not there was an actual murder. However, given the fragmented and piece-meal characteristics of her memory, it was likely symbolic or non-declarative traumatic memory. Certainly, it was not stable enough to hold up under a police interrogation.

Debbie spoke about the abuse as if it had nothing to do with her. Everything about Debbie had a washed-out faded quality. This is not uncommon with DID patients, particularly when the alter speaking is commenting on another alter's experience.

In our sessions, we never moved much deeper than dealing with her day-to-day living problems, including agoraphobia. She was dutiful in her visits to her formerly abusive father, who was now a resident in a nursing home. She expressed great fear around these obligatory visits, even though her father had become incapacitated in many ways by Alzheimer's disease.

I did not engage the alters in therapy. They were not presenting any problems with her then-current day-to-day functioning.

During her five years in therapy, Debbie did not have any more time-loss or memory lapses, and she became much calmer. As her life became relatively stable, Debbie seemed to be satisfied with the limited changes she had achieved in therapy.

It is possible that she could not envisage a goal to reach for that went beyond dealing with those day-to-day challenges. It may be that Debbie's system did not feel ready to process further trauma or that it did not then need to do so. In either circumstance, the therapeutic alliance was left intact so as to be available when and if called upon.

Therapeutic Keys

With Debbie and others like her, the goals of DID treatment may need to be scaled down to modest, realistic expectations. Some patients are satisfied with a life absent disabling symptoms. Most people in their late 50s may be content in a life that lacks stress. Debbie had no ambition other than to keep her status quo. The therapist must wait until the patient is ready to work directly with the root of the DID. Do not push. The therapist must accept that this may never happen, and be satisfied to provide the temporary support requested.

Alletta - Limited Success

I treated Alletta, a talented artist in her late 50s, for six years, seeing her about every two to three weeks. She had no memory of her childhood before the age of 12, but remembered being abused by her father throughout her teenage years. After spending 20 years in treatment with ten different therapists, she settled into a life rigidly controlled by an austere diet and grueling physical exercise. She adopted this regimen as a way to keep herself safe: By remaining skeletally thin, she felt that she was keeping herself physically unattractive. She cut and slashed her arms, as well as burning them with cigarettes.

Alletta's her list of symptoms included incapacitating panic attacks as well as bouts of self-mutilation. She also suffered from agoraphobia and borderline anorexia nervosa. Shortly before coming in to see me, she had stopped her heavy drinking. She had already made a self-diagnosis of DID, and was aware of 17 clearly defined alters. Each alter had a specific function. All of them knew of each other.

Being an accomplished artist, Alletta used drawings to show me her experience of abuse. Putting an abuse experience in a drawing gave her the advantage of being fully in control of how the drawing evolved. This can be a powerful way to process trauma.

She usually came in with stacks of drawings. These drawings showed a startling realism. For example, one image was that of a sad young child stuck in a confined space with a big man with a large penis. The image had the correct perspective, as if it was a photograph taken with a wide-angle lens. The drawing seemed consistent with the perspective a four year old girl. As with many others, Alletta was first diagnosed as having DID during art therapy.

She showed me some fascinating photos from the early 60s of her family in Europe. One was a photograph of her father, a high ranking and well decorated military man. He was smartly dressed in his uniform, attending some function in the presence of royalty. This was not surprising as, in my practice, I had repeatedly seen how normal and highly respectable appearances may mask a deep pathology.

She spoke about the abuse as if telling a story that did not concern her. She talked about it like Debbie, in a disconnected way, rather than like Doris, who spoke about the trauma without flashbacks but with an emotional connection. This lack of affect in narrating the experience of abuse is a sign of dissociation, in keeping with the diagnosis of DID when other features of fragmentation are present.

Alletta's system of multiplicity was deeply entrenched. A "dictator" inside managed the chaos. I tried to soften his tyrannical control, but he would not budge. I had difficulty directly communicating with any alter. There was a strong internal force that was maintaining the multiplicity system. Even so, keeping in mind that the alters were all listening, I continued therapy by speaking to the patient as a collective of multiplicity.

Alletta did improve in many ways. As a result of therapy, she stopped cutting and burning herself. She told me that she had become less housebound and, according to her friends, she looked must better. She was able to take a bus to my office, instead of relying on her husband to drive her every time. She gathered enough courage to visit her home country with him. She had progressed to the point that she could undergo a physical examination by a doctor. She even decided on her own to quit smoking and succeeded.

The biggest threat to her stability in future would be physical, as she kept herself on a dangerously low caloric intake and a high intensity exercise program. If her arthritis worsened with age, she would no longer be able to do the punishing daily run up and down the mountains behind her house. Her desire to stay underweight might push her into further reduction of her caloric intake, with dangerous health consequences.

I consider Alletta's case a limited success. As a therapist, I was stone-walled by the alter functioning as a dictator. This alter appeared to have set limits, binding the other alters and preventing them from engaging with me. When Alletta stopped therapy at my retirement, her new-found stability seemed precarious. It was clear that she could easily topple under the weight of new stressors.

Therapeutic Keys

When working with a DID system that is unwilling to allow engagement with alters due to one overriding controlling alter, the therapist must remain patient and do what they can to maintain the no-doubt fragile beginnings of a therapeutic alliance. The hope is that through remaining open and available, should the other alters decide to engage in therapy, they will remember that it is indeed possible to work with a therapist that understands DID. Had I not retired, perhaps progress might have continued to the point that the dictator would have permitted the necessary therapeutic engagement. That will remain uncertain.

Working with dictatorial alters is always difficult. As seen in many of these case histories, progress often comes over long periods of time that may include gaps in therapy. Hence, the importance of having an open time-frame view of treatment.

Mary - Chaotic Behaviors Impacting Therapy

Mary was a 19-year old patient whose chaotic life interfered with therapy. Her parents brought her to the hospital Emergency. She was assessed by the on-call psychiatrist who suspected her to be suffering from DID. However, he did not name DID as either the primary or even a differential diagnosis. Instead, he looked at her multiple behavior problems of drinking, drug abuse and chaotic relationships, and then chose an unhelpful diagnosis of borderline personality disorder.

She had been on the waiting list to see me, but because she ended up in the Emergency, she jumped the queue. I discharged her from the Emergency and she came to see me a few days later. The psychologist she had been seeing said to me, "I have always been skeptical of the diagnosis of DID. However, she would become aggressive and abusive in a therapy session, only to return nice and polite the next time with no memory of the last session. In one session, she became a child sitting on the floor. In another session, she was acting like a child singing nursery rhymes."

The Mary I first saw was cool and intellectual. She had been seeing a psychologist for eight months, and they had spoken about DID. She talked about and used simple names for the eight dissociated parts inside her for the sake of communication.

She was not interested in showing her alters to me, nor were the alters ready to show themselves. One was angry. Another was college-material, interested in the works of Edgar Allan Poe. One was an organizer in charge of day-to-day affairs. One was sexually preoccupied and exploitative. One was given to swearing, arguing, and prostituting for money. Of the other alters who were also present, one was extremely cynical and wanted to sabotage anything good happening to the host.

I saw her intermittently over three years, but we never formed a sustained therapeutic alliance. I believe therapy was unsuccessful as we were unable to overcome or co-opt the saboteur alter.

Mary's life was interrupted by numerous incidents. She jumped from job to job, sometimes working two jobs. She tried college, but lasted only a few months. When her mother kicked her out of the house, she moved in with a prostitute friend whose boyfriend wanted to have "kinky" sex with her. She had many explanations for the long time gaps between seeing me.

When she was reasonably well settled on social assistance, something or someone was always there to restart the social turmoil. She would go back to her abusive boyfriend or an alter would come out to involve her in yet another abusive relationship. She even ended up in court for drunken assault.

She usually needed two jobs to make ends meet, but was unable to keep even one. With her job record and grade ten education, her job opportunities were limited. Crises followed one after another; a motor vehicle accident, a six hour stay at the hospital Emergency, an insurance claim, a court case, and then a shoplifting arrest.

While she said she appreciated my help, she resented having to take two buses and one train trip to see me. I was unable to find a therapist closer to her home willing to take her on as a patient. Against all odds, she never missed an appointment. Her longest stable period was ten weeks. At that time, she was living alone and working as a telemarketer.

After these three years of intermittent therapy, she quit. In her last session, she said she would set three goals:

1. Stop prostituting

2. Stop using alcohol and drugs

3. Lose ten pounds

Mary's case history highlights that fact that a patient who, despite obstacles, still goes to therapy and never misses an appointment, must feel an imperative to heal.

Therapeutic Keys

Consider the inclusion of goal 3: From any conventional point of view, losing ten pounds is not in the same class as stopping prostituting or addition, yet for that alter, it is of equal importance, if not more.

One must deal directly with the issues that specific alters have, if they are causing conflict and disharmony. When speaking to an alter whose focus is losing ten pounds, telling that alter her concern is dwarfed by other issues such as prostituting or addiction will not be helpful. That alter may not see those issues as relevant to her in any way.

Despite such clear motivation to heal, Mary never really made progress in therapy. This illustrates ways that therapeutic progress in DID treatment may be undermined by a saboteur alter. Given the wisdom of hindsight, more energetic engagement with the saboteur alter might have resulted in a different outcome.

Sharon - Intransigent Alters

Alters may be so resistant that they do not allow a single crack of light into the system. Some alters who enjoy their freedom and autonomy see no reason for change. They act out, have some wild fun, and leave the host or some other alters to clean up the mess after they have disappeared. In other cases, paranoid and extremely suspicious alters may be too mistrustful to allow genuine engagement in psychotherapy. Alters who are extremely entrenched in their own ways may resist the development of any therapeutic alliance.

Sharon was a highly fragmented DID patient. She was quite dissociative, with many episodes of time-loss. She would get side-tracked each time therapy seemed to be progressing. A kindly retired social-worker took Sharon into her home, providing her food and lodging.

One fun-loving alter caused her to disappear for periods of time, running off to a nearby town where she got mixed up at random with unhelpful people.

This alter behaved like a delinquent teenager. She liked to play billiards and hitch rides on motorcycles. She brought home undesirables. I was unable to enlist the cooperation of the delinquent alter to join in the therapeutic effort for the common good of the whole system.

She missed therapy appointments on numerous occasions as she went on adventures all over the province: Vancouver Island, Kelowna, the Sunshine Coast. She went wherever her motorcycle friends would take her. Yet she always came back crying, asking me to take her back for psychotherapy.

For six years Sharon showed up off and on in my appointment book. Eventually, I refused to take her back. I realized that there had been no progress and likely no hope of any to come. By then, the kindly retired social worker had also asked Sharon to leave her home. It only took this one intransigent alter to destroy her chance for recovery.

One day in deep winter, my secretary saw Sharon shivering in the cold, begging for money on the street. That was about 18 months after I took her name off my appointment book.

Therapeutic Keys

Given Sharon's pattern of missed appointments, I am not confident that her fate would have changed even had we continued therapy. Without an effective therapeutic alliance, disruptive alters that cannot be induced to engage, even indirectly, in therapy will undermine the possibility of healing. As a therapist, one must be prepared for such great and painful disappointments.

Charles - Inability to Face Multiplicity

It takes great courage to face the multiplicity confirmed by a diagnosis of DID. The host may be overwhelmed by the failure of self-control implied by episodes of time-loss. In addition, many alters within DID patients do not accept the idea of sharing one body with other alters. Like a child who feels sidelined by a new sibling, most alters want to feel special. They want the freedom to remain separate and autonomous, not having to think about the good of the collective.

Charles was one of less than a dozen male DID patients with whom I worked in my 40 years of psychiatric practice. Male DIDs are supposedly rare. The male to female ratio is said to be about one to six. Charles came to see me because he was unhappy with the diagnosis of DID he had received from his psychologist.

A middle-aged, single man with a good job, Charles had been seeing a therapist for over a year. Apart from the fact that he had little memory prior to the age of eight, there was nothing unusual in his background or current social history. His parents and siblings all had good professional careers. He and his siblings were brought up mainly by a nanny, whom he remembered fondly.

Without prompting, in our first interview he described hallmark symptoms of DID. In his own assessment, he was suffering from headaches at least 30% of the time, and felt spaced out most of the time. He would have frequent time-loss episodes at home of up to three hours. Afterwards, he could not account for what he had done. Sometimes, he later learned that that he had been out of the house.

In one significant time-loss episode, he had to ask the police to locate his car for him, having lost more than 24 hours of conscious time. When he found his car, he discovered that half of the gas in the tank was gone. Furthermore, half of a package of cigarettes was found in his car, even though he was a non-smoker.

He frequently found money missing from his wallet and clothing in his closet that did not accord with his taste. On several occasions, strangers he could not remember meeting had approached him, greeting him with unfamiliar names. He heard inner voices talking to and about him. There were pages in his diary missing, ripped off, or with lines crossed out. He also had episodes of explosive anger followed by amnesia, episodes he knew about only because friends had told him afterwards.

He only saw me four times. Knowing that he did not accept the psychologist's DID diagnosis, I delayed confirming it. I think he had confirmed the diagnosis for himself during our sessions. Not many people can accept that another part of the self is operating outside one's consciousness.

Therapeutic Keys

Sometimes, the proper diagnosis is simply too difficult for a patient to accept. Knowing that a patient has such difficulties, and that they may be insurmountable, the therapist might take the approach of noting the difficulty and inviting the host and alters to take their time to process the information. Most importantly, if the patient decides to discontinue therapy, make it clear that that the door is always open to the host or any alter that wishes to re-engage.

Engaging Multiple Personalities – Volume 1

Chapter 11   Laura - My Last Patient, Summary on Treatment

This case history concerns my last DID patient before retirement. I have included it in some detail so as to provide a summary, a basic template for the treatment of DID. It also illustrates the problem of there being a dearth of psychiatrists willing to treat DID.

About four months before I was slated to retire, I received a referral from a psychiatrist in Victoria, the provincial capital of British Columbia. It is a few hours' journey from there to my office in Vancouver, involving a 90 minute ferry crossing and two bus rides. The referring psychiatrist had a long well-established practice in Victoria. However, it appeared that he had been unsuccessful in his search for a local therapist to refer this DID patient. This was the first time he had referred a patient to me.

Laura was a 38 year old woman with little money living on an off-shore island. She had limited treatment options and seemed urgent in her desire to find a therapist to treat her DID. The diagnosis had been confirmed by two psychiatrists before this. Apparently, I was the only psychiatrist she could find who might take her on as a patient.

I had some difficulty in justifying acceptance of her as my patient given that it would only be for 4 months, especially as she was living quite far away. Her willingness to do this, even knowing of my impending retirement, attests to the lack of trained therapists that were willing to treat people with DID available in two of the biggest cities in the province.

Following her initial DID diagnosis, Laura had engaged in treatment for two years with a psychologist. Since she'd had to pay the psychologist privately, therapy stopped when she ran out of funds. She then saw a social worker for three and a half years, stopping when the social worker relocated to another city.

Both psychiatrists had confirmed a DID diagnosis, but would not take up ongoing therapy with her. One cited his "lack of expertise in the treatment of DID." The other told Laura that it would be harmful to engage in dialogue with the alters, as that would "encourage dissociative defenses." As to the second rationale, Laura's previous therapy had shown her that engagement in dialogue with the alters was essential to making progress toward healing.

Laura's father had been a university professor. He had sexually abused her early in her life. This continued until she was 15. The abuse then came to a sudden halt. Her mother wavered between fluttering sympathy and denial. She would sometimes believe Laura's story of abuse, and at other times completely dismiss her.

Laura presented with typical symptoms of dissociation and fragmentation, the chaotic result of having many inner parts along with the PTSD of traumatized alters. The separation into parts had caused an inner civil war, which led to much dysfunction in her daily life. One alter wanted to hurt or kill another, ignoring the fact that they shared the same body.

There was a ten year period during which Laura was successfully engaged in a career that was a customarily a man's job. It demanded heavy physical fitness. She felt safe and secure, enjoying her physical prowess and the company of burly men.

This sense of security collapsed several years before seeing me when she started having PTSD symptoms and being disturbed by intrusive abuse memories. Something must have triggered opening the floodgates of disturbing emotions and traumatic memories. She lost her health, career and financial security.

She started having flashbacks. She was in a distressing and sorrowful state when she arrived at my office. She was trembling, cowering, and shivering. Her voice was small and shaky. Laura alluded to memories of past abuse that had not been processed or encoded in explicit, narrative form. These non-declarative memories were expressed through her body, which presented as a frightened child. It was hard to imagine that she previously had worked in a well-paying physically demanding job.

Helping someone recover from trauma requires teaching the survivor that she can observe the traumatic event and place it in its proper time and place in the past. It happened "then and there", while the survivor is in the safe sanctuary of "here and now."

Teaching the survivor to feel safe is the basic groundwork needed to overcome the power of the overwhelming past intruding into the present. Because they have lost the capacity to recognize or register the feeling of safety, survivors with undigested traumatic memory have to learn feeling safe from the very beginning of therapy.

Laura also believed that she had been ritually abused. She mentioned a very hazy memory involving her father leading some sort of ritual. She even had a foggy memory that a man might have been killed at one of these gatherings. I did not feel the need to challenge or discount what she said. As the purpose of therapy is to help patients free themselves from the clutches of the past and move more easily to the present moment, I did not need to take her story as literally accurate. It could be just as easily seen as a mixture of non-declarative memory coupled with metaphors for her experience of powerlessness and fear.

I did not ask for more details or clarification of the ritual abuse. The patient, as a traumatized victim, would likely experience such a request as judgmental cross-examination or mere voyeuristic interest.

I have always considered it unnecessary to seek details when patients presented to me past abuse experiences, whether they had a ritual aspect or not. It is necessary to be prepared to engage with any alter that might bring up such memories, but it is always best to let the patient/alter take the lead. Laura needed to be acknowledged and understood. She needed to express that she had been through extraordinary painful and fearful experiences of unspeakable horror, and to know that she would be heard.

There was no reason to go into any detail of Laura's history or current psychological disturbances. It was clear that she had been severely traumatized by incest. It was also clear that, after many years of protection by means of the dissociative process, the memories had broken through the defenses. Filled with flashbacks and internal strife, her life was no longer the same.

She had a few years of therapy that had not been brought to completion. I tried to design a program of self-healing for her with the intention of starting her on a course of recovery. I hoped she would be able to find a therapist who could at least see her at regular monthly intervals on a supportive basis to supervise her self-directed therapy after my retirement.

Taking key points of treatment plans I had used for other DID patients, I started to give Laura instructions. She would only have eight hours of therapy with me. Laura was ready with her pen and paper to take notes. Therapy was organized around two principles:

1) The treatment of the chaos of the inner family, and

2) The gentle de-stressing and working through of PTSD held by some alters.

I firmly believe that all therapy contains a large measure of self-healing. DID patients need to develop the confidence to take up a measure of self-directed therapy. It is necessary for the alters to cooperate and work as a team. The therapist must encourage the patient's system to do this. It is further desirable for the system to assign one alter the responsibility of being an inner-therapist, and to follow a written guideline to help maintain focus.

Some patients come in with part of that foundation in place, such as Victoria. The therapist must then build upon that foundation. For those that come in without much, or even any of that foundation, the task is far more difficult.

Treating the Chaos of the Inner Family

To treat the internal chaos, one must teach the alters that they share the same body. One must encourage them to learn to live together in cooperation. They have to compromise with and tolerate each other in order to have a decent life. In a sense, it is teaching them that they will all do best by functioning as a cohesive unit. None will get 100% of what they want, but they will all get acknowledgment, understanding and as much of what they each want as the intact system can provide.

With Laura, I went so far as demonstrating this point of sharing the same body by holding her right little finger and pinching gently, asking if "Jane" and "June" could feel the same squeeze. This kind of touch test might seem childish. Actually, it is more correctly seen as child-like. That child-like approach has tremendous power in DID treatment because many of the alters are children.

Learning that each alter experiences that same squeeze helps break down the amnestic barrier separating the alters from each other and the host. Note that there may be alters that simply do not feel the bodily sensation as do the others. In this aspect of the therapy, teaching is involved and the therapist needs to be directive.

Therapists need to remember that the amnestic barrier was created for a reason, and cannot simply be attacked from without. Gently invite its dissolution indirectly through the therapy, by engaging the host and each of the alters as they present. Before therapists can work effectively with alters, they need to establish a therapeutic alliance with them. Some alters are reasonably receptive, but others can be extremely resistant or disruptive. If I was the coach of a soccer team that had a disruptive player, I would invite him out and talk to him. In working with DID, a difficult alter may require similar individual attention. That attention is necessary to encourage disruptive individuals to go with the group, as part of a team focused on a common goal. Fortunately, the delinquent alter is usually malleable and ready to change. Such an alter is often simply in need of acknowledgment as the predicate to joining the group.

Working with alters as a group can take the form of a community meeting. Imagine a group session with an angry, obstructive and narcissistic member who refuses to participate, who tries to sabotage efforts to foster community, and who neither can nor should be expelled from the group. Therapy is likely to be the first time that alter has been asked to consider others in the system. Therefore, it is critical that the therapist communicate that joining the group means that the alter will still be respected and valued in their own right.

It is not uncommon for some angry alters to express the view that they simply do not care if everyone dies, including themselves. Avoiding any acknowledgment of such alters is a critical mistake, an extremely dangerous one. It is often the angry ones that have enabled the system to survive the aftermath of abuse. Engaging them directly is the safest and most direct path to transitioning their rage into community protection, as part of a whole team mentality.

Some alters are very frightened if the word integration is mentioned during therapy. They see this as an attempt to annihilate them. I usually stress that members of the inner household can keep their individuality so long as they wish or need to. Often, as the host makes progress, some alters recede enough that they no longer obstruct the functioning of the whole, while others just disappear.

Unlike the dramatic epiphanies depicted in movies about DID, integration is a gradual process whereby the differences among the alters soften and diminish. This occurs as the patient learns to cope with stressors and crises without uncontrollably switching into alters. In fact, what often occurs is that the patient becomes able to draw upon the different strengths of the alters without requiring separation through amnestic barriers. In other words, their protective functions can be accessed as a matter of co-consciousness rather than through the chaos of uncontrollable flashbacks. Complete integration is therefore not the necessary mark of healing as cooperative co-consciousness may be of equivalent benefit.

Keeping in mind our very limited time, I concentrated on training Laura to have community meetings to bring the alters together, and to foster a sense of group cohesion. As quickly as possible, I tried to break down obstinate individualism, promoting a sense of group spirit, and mutual support.

Laura paid full attention and took notes. Having prepared her as completely as possible under the time constraints, I hoped that what she had learned was consolidated and supported her healing.

Treating the Unprocessed Trauma in Complex PTSD

The usual PTSD patient, who has experienced a single traumatic event, generally does not experience the pervasive low self-esteem, guilt and resulting interpersonal dysfunction that follow the betrayal of trust and destruction of personal boundaries experienced in incest. For this reason, Judith Herman[33] proposed the term Complex PTSD to denote the condition that results from chronic or long-

---

[33]Herman J. (1992) Complex PTSD: A Syndrome in Survivors of Prolonged and Repeated Trauma. Journal of Traumatic Stress Vol.5 No.3.

term exposure to emotional trauma over which a victim has little or no control, and from which there is little or no hope of escape. Examples include the kind of repeated childhood emotional, physical and sexual abuse that Laura experienced. Incest, which usually lasts for years, is a particularly malignant long-term entrapment.

A victim of childhood incest will commonly exhibit a constellation of social problems and physical symptoms in addition to those mentioned above: anxiety, depression, somatization, dissociation, eating disorders, sexual problems, and substance abuse as well as suicidal ideation and attempts.[34] Abuse by caretakers they are dependent upon puts children in an impossible double-bind. One of the few options for survival is the creation of escape routes in their minds. Some dissociate to such a degree that they go on to develop full-blown DID. Most of the DID patients I treated had been traumatized for a prolonged period in childhood.[35] In the absence of a therapist, the self-healing path of a DID patient can make use of extensive journal writing. Journal writing can effectively enact a therapeutic dissociation, a split into an observing ego and an experiencing ego. By dividing the page with a vertical line in the middle, one side can ask questions and play the part of a listening therapist while on the other side, the survivor can reveal the event, either by writing or drawing. By putting these on paper, there is a strong suggestion that the overflow of emotion can be controlled. The therapist side can always physically close the book to declare an intermission in the session, or place the memory on a temporary hold.

----

[34]John Briere (1992), p.196.   Child Abuse Trauma: Theory and Treatment of the Lasting Effects. SAGE publications Newbury Park London New Delhi.
[35]Jennifer Freyd (1998) Betrayal Trauma: The Logic of Forgetting Childhood Abuse. Harvard University Press

Patients must learn to know when they are ready to venture inward and explore more deeply. They need to be taught and actually experience the key fact that processing the trauma in order to gain some sense of mastery over it is <u>not</u> the same as reliving it. It is also not the same as just talking about it. It is about touching the wound lightly, experiencing and recognizing the discrepancy between one's heightened physiological arousal and the actual situation happening right now in a safe place, where there is no threat. The education is about understanding timing; when to start and when to stop.

I suggested that Laura use a ritualized procedure involving body posture and movement techniques for stopping self-therapy sessions. When flashbacks arise in self-therapy, this ritual sequence enables the disengagement from the past trauma – thus freeing the mind from the immediacy of the emotional turmoil that is locked in the body. The ceremony consisted of opening and closing the journal, putting it in a drawer, and going immediately into a physically demanding task such as a yoga posture or series of push-ups. Ultimately, learning to experience safety and security forms the basis of processing past trauma. Since Laura had only a limited number of hours before the termination of therapy with me, the remaining hours were devoted to teaching her grounding exercises. This work was aimed toward helping her to reclaim control over her body.

A good therapeutic test is to simply ask a patient to sit still, close her eyes and pay attention to her breathing. Observation of the patient during the next few minutes can yield much information on their mental state. For Laura, in pursuing her self-therapy, such a therapeutic test was important. Attention to the breath enhances skills of self-observation and affective regulation. Through this, I hoped that Laura would be able to use this technique to interrupt unwelcome flashbacks.

If there is a good therapeutic alliance, the patient feels the support of the therapist and may then be able to direct her attention to her center core. In the absence of a therapist, I encouraged Laura to assign the role to an inner-helper and to have that inner-helper provide the support. If all went well, a feedback loop of self-reinforced calmness could begin. Learning to attend to one's own breath becomes a very grounding experience for those vulnerable to the ambush of intense emotional flashbacks.

During the 16 hours I spent with Laura, spread over eight sessions, I spent a substantial part of that time teaching Laura to breathe slowly, to pay attention to her body, and to experience what it meant for the body to feel comfortable and relaxed. Most of our sessions were focused on the present state of being, not ruminating over past events.

Re-tracing past traumas and injustices without processing, simply carves deeper and deeper grooves in the psyche. It does not allow relief, and does not have any therapeutic value for traumatized patients. This was repeatedly emphasized so that Laura would internalize that she had to first learn to feel comfortable and safe through her breath work, before venturing into more directly working with the trauma.

I taught Laura a few strategies which she could apply therapy in her self-directed therapy:

1. Assign one of her alters to be an "inner therapist," similar to how I described working with Victoria.

2. Make use of journaling as a form of therapy.

3.   Pay attention to her body and make sure she practiced good muscular, cardiovascular, and stretching exercises.

4.   Pay attention to spiritual health. Going through treatment for DID is a very lonely task. Patients who do not have a sense of getting extra support from God or a higher power are easily disappointed and discouraged. All my patients who did better than average cultivated a healthy spiritual life. Practice breath work until she feels the self-soothing quality of it before starting trauma therapy.

My final instructions to Laura are summarized below:

"Therapy does not mean digging up the past. You have been severely traumatized for many years in early childhood. Whatever happened has taken away your personal power so that even thinking about it terrorizes you, makes you helpless, and gives you a sense of being out of control. What you need to focus on is the tangible palpable sensation of safety and security of the here and now. Use whatever you have to generate that comfortable feeling, in a natural way rather than using alcohol or drugs. When you have this sense of safety and security, past traumatic events will lose their power to take over your body. Your presence, the here and now, is the greatest gift that is given to you. I hope that my time spent with Melissa [one of Laura's alters], has demonstrated to everyone inside that you can do much of the therapy yourself."

Laura's circumstances had put her in a desperate situation: She had to spend the better part of a day to travel to see me for each two-hour session. From the entire pool of psychiatrists in three major cities in British Columbia, I was the only one she could find willing to take her on for treatment of DID, and that was unfortunately limited by my impending retirement.

I wrote a brief report to the referring psychiatrist explaining what I had done. I expressed my view that even if she could not find a psychiatrist that would treat her DID in her home city, it was important that she find a therapist to see her on at least a monthly basis to support her self-directed therapeutic work.

I have no idea how she fared after the last session, which took place in the closing days of my practice. My fervent hope is that she did indeed find a therapist who would see her and reinforce what I had taught her in our short time together.

Therapeutic Keys

Treating a person with DID means developing an attitude of compassion and respect toward the alters whenever and however they emerge, whether it be shyly, boldly, flirtatiously or aggressively. Successful treatment of the alters does not mean eradication of them or of their functions. Encouraging an alter to take on the role of inner therapist is very important. A capable therapist inside can be guided, mentored and trained to use the dissociation as an asset in self-treatment.

Following successful treatment, when alters do emerge at times, they no longer paralyze the system. They come out at an appropriate moment, such as an assertive alter appearing when being assertive is helpful. In that way, they are cooperating and coordinating in the daily functioning of the system.

AFTERWORD

DID is a complex disorder. It is true that many patients are difficult to treat. Many psychiatrists have chosen to ignore this condition for far too long, to the detriment and suffering of many so afflicted. Healing is possible. While some may not respond to treatment, others do derive partial relief from their suffering. For some, therapy will bring back their previous level of functioning. For others, therapy will allow them to flourish even more.

For therapists to take the position that they should "forget about the past, just treat the manifest depression of the present" is a dangerous error of over-simplification. This resulted in the therapists seeing and aiming to treat only the depression, and often only through medications. Time and again, there were patients who did not improve because their therapists, relying on such a mechanistic view, maintained this enormous blind spot.

We can do better. We may not always be able to tell which seeds will germinate, but survivors of childhood trauma, and the enormity of their numbers is beyond dispute, deserve an opportunity to heal and recover.

Appendix 1   Dissociation as an Asset

Dissociation is not always pathological. For example, a surgeon in the middle of a nasty divorce must remain able to concentrate in the operating room. The act of separating the ordinary stream of divorce related thoughts from the task of surgery at hand requires effective dissociation.

Without conscious effort, many DID persons utilize their dissociative abilities to enhance their work. Teachers with DID can be exceptionally perceptive and sensitive to their students' difficulties because their young alters easily tune into the students' needs. Similarly, a therapist with alters can be readily attuned to their patients in therapeutic work. Some DID persons are able to function quite adequately in their particular work situations, despite the presence of a host of alters within.

One of my patients operated a summer camp. She had exceptionally capable and sensitive alters who were effectively like child psychologists. Her acumen in spotting pathology and handling difficult children was often marveled at by professionals to whom these children were referred for consultation. They were quite astonished that she picked up pathologies among her campers well before anyone else noticed anything amiss, including their parents.

Many DID patients have alters with tremendous skills. Herschel Walker, a great American athlete, is a famous DID person. He became a professional football player, martial artist, and an Olympic bobsled competitor. Early in life, his dissociation enabled him to survive emotional abuse, bullying at school, and isolation in his early childhood. It also allowed him to develop his athletic skills so that by 14 he made it to the school football team and by 17 he was named the national high school scholar-athlete of the year. [36]

Robert Oxnam clearly recognized advantages in his DID that helped his teaching position in China's Beijing University.[37]

> "I came to realize that our inner MPD structure offered me an unusual advantage as a teacher. Once multiple personalities are able to interact internally, it is easier for them to operate empathetically in a multicultural context. While one of us was talking, the other two were listening and watching, making it easier to sense feelings. When discussing international issues, I was surprised that I could instinctively sense not only American reactions but also Chinese reactions... In short, this old professor learned far more by listening to his own students than they learned by listening to his lectures. And since this professor just happened to have multiple personalities, he found that Bobby (one alter) and Wanda (another alter) were often more perceptive about 'Chinese thinking' than he was. As a result

---

[36]Walker, H. *Breaking Free,* Touchstone and Howard Books. A Division of Simon & Schuster, Inc. New York, NY. 2008.

[37]Oxnam, R. B. *A Fractured Mind: My life with Multiple Personality Disorder,* Hyperion, New York, NY. 2005 p. 251 Oxnam is a China scholar and former president of the Asia Society. He led financial-cultural tours of China for Bill Gates, Warren Buffett and former US president George H.W. Bush.

my MPD side and my Asia side came together in a splendid moment at Beijing University."

The single most significant benefit of dissociation in a DID patient is the ability to assign an alter, or actually split off an alter, to act as a therapist, as seen with my patient Victoria (Chapter 7). Victoria's successful treatment, while living hundreds of kilometers from my office, was only possible because of an able inner therapist. The total number of hours of therapy required to heal was less than 60, despite a severe pathology that included years of depression and many hospitalizations. This example of the observing ego fragment successfully doing therapy on the experiencing ego fragment is unique to DID therapy.

Ruth (Chapter 5) utilized the same mechanism to accelerate her psychotherapeutic process. In DID therapy, the therapists must take advantage of this unique propensity in their patients and, when appropriate, promote the utilization of such inner therapist(s).

A DID patient may heal to the point where the alters coexist in a harmonious manner, but without full integration. Such a coalition may be a desirable therapeutic outcome. So long as they have learned to live in a harmonious manner, alters with special skills are able to come out when and as needed without conflict.

Engaging Multiple Personalities – Appendices

Appendix 2:   Debates, and Controversies, False Memory, and PTSD

There has been ongoing debate on many issues related to MPD. Foremost is debate on the notion that early childhood trauma leads to dissociation, and that dissociated fragmentation of the mind can appear as the different identities shown or reported by patients. However, all these are related to the central debate, which is whether MPD (DID) exists as a legitimate disorder or is the result of therapy suggested or implanted by therapists.

The controversies that have clouded discussion of MPD for decades came into sharp focus in 1992 when Harold Merskey, then a Professor of Psychiatry at the University of Western Ontario, wrote an article in the British Journal of Psychiatry entitled: "The Manufacture of Personalities: The production of Multiple Personality Disorder."[38] He pointed out that unprecedented numbers of cases of MPD were diagnosed since 1957, mainly in North America. This was the year that *"The Three Faces of Eve"* was released in movie theaters. He argued that the so-called personalities frequently appeared as an adjunct to hypnosis, and could be explained by iatrogenesis - a false condition developed in therapy.

Three years later, Merskey followed up with an editorial in the same journal questioning the relationship between MPD and early childhood sexual abuse as well as the idea of recovered memories. Since treatment for MPD patients is often linked to a return of lost memories of early

---

[38]Merskey H. *The Manufacture of Personalities: The production of Multiple Personality Disorder.* Br J Psychiatry: 1992; 160:327-340.

sexual abuse, his editorial was entitled: "Multiple Personality Disorder and False Memory Syndrome."[39] He pointed out one survey in Canada showing that 41% of psychiatrists had never seen a case of DID. He failed to note that this means 59% of psychiatrists presumably had seen cases of DID. He further points out that the same survey found that 68% of psychiatrists had never made a diagnosis of DID, again failing to note the corollary - that 32% had.

In another survey among families who had joined the False Memory Foundation in the USA, 18% of the alleged victims of childhood abuse also reported satanic ritual abuse. The inference made in quoting this survey was that since the claim of satanic ritual abuse was allegedly groundless, then the childhood sexual abuse claimed by the victims was likely false memory.[40]

In 2004, Merskey published a review article in the Canadian Journal of Psychiatry on the same subject. This time he did not mince words, entitling the paper "The Persistence of Folly: A Critical Examination of Dissociative Identity Disorder."[41] [42] In this way, Merskey continued to raise doubts as to the appropriateness of retaining the

---

[39]Merskey H. *Multiple Personality Disorder and False Memory Syndrome. British J Psychiatry* :1996;166: 281-283.

[40]For further discussion of Satanic ritual abuse and false memory, see *Engaging Multiple Personalities Volume 2* (publication pending)

[41]Piper, A., Merskey, H. *The Persistence of Folly: A Critical Examination of Dissociative Identity Disorder. Part I. The Excesses of an Improbable Concept.* Can J Psychiatry 2004; 49:592–600.

[42] Piper, A.,Merskey, H. *The Persistence of Folly: Critical Examination of Dissociative Identity Disorder Part II. The Defence and Decline of Multiple Personality or Dissociative Identity Disorder.* Can J Psychiatry 2004; 49:678-683

diagnostic label of MPD/DID in official classifications.

Among my own group of DID patients, I found a similar percentage of them reporting satanic ritual abuse. However, therapy is not beholden to proving or disproving such reports as factual statements. I conceived such reports as metaphoric expressions of unspeakable terror in the hands of abusers who demanded secrecy, who were endowed with authority, and who possessed almost supernatural power over the child. One must not infer a need to act as a judge concerning the SRA. The most important point is that abuse did happen and you are seeing the consequences. One must act as a therapist for a traumatized patient, not a judge or jury as to the specific details of the abuse.

Debates continue to swirl around the legitimacy of DID as a diagnosis. Joel Paris of McGill University's Department of Psychiatry, argued that DID was a medical fad, and should never have been included in the fifth edition of the Diagnostic and Statistical Manual of Mental Disorders (DSM-5)[43]. Paris is the current chief editor of the Canadian Journal of Psychiatry. As such, his influence is widespread.

However, letters to the editor in the April 2013 issue of the same journal included rebuttals by practitioners from Puerto Rico, New Zealand, Australia, and South Africa, who objected strenuously to Paris's claims about the "supposedly dwindling fad of DID and dissociative disorders." These rebuttals stated that Paris's views do not acknowledge "current peer-reviewed international

---

[43]Paris J. Journal of Nervous and Mental Diseases. 2012; 200 (12): 1007-1135.

research"[44]

Another letter by Bethany Brand and colleagues[45] also objected to Paris's argument. This letter stated that "his (Paris's) point of view is incorrect and outmoded. It is the so-called false-memory, iatrogenesis (iatrogenic) model of dissociative disorders that is the fallen fad, buried under the weight of rigorous data that contradict it."

This debate is by no means limited to Canada. Experts from major universities and medical schools such as Stanford and Johns Hopkins in the USA are likewise involved in such debates. One must not lose sight of the fact that this debate is focused on a well-established disorder that has always been officially recognized in international diagnostic manuals.

My question to these ivory tower academics who deny the reality of DID is, "How would you treat patients like Joan and Ruth (in Chapters 1 and 3), who had wasted their time for years suffering from disability until treatment was initiated and applied to the alters?" The proof is in the pudding, not in empty theoretical debates.

---

[44]Martínez-Taboas, Alfonso PhD; Dorahy, Martin PhD; Sar, Vedat MD; Middleton, Warwick MD; Krüger, Christa MD. *Growing Not Dwindling: International Research on the Worldwide Phenomenon of Dissociative Disorders* Journal of Nervous & Mental Disease 2013; 201 (4): 353–354.

[45]Brand, B., Loewenstein, R. J., Spiegel, D. *Disinformation About Dissociation: Dr. Joel Paris's Notions About Dissociative Identity Disorder.* Journal of Nervous & Mental Disease 2013; 201(4): 354–356.

False Memory Syndrome

There is ancillary debate on the veracity of the early childhood abuse as claimed by patients when such memories return, sometimes during therapy. Misguided therapists, delving into the details of their patients' histories, indiscriminately laid the blame on childhood abusers. These therapists were accused of implanting and suggesting false histories of abuse on their patients.

Some of these therapists thought that by taking the abusers to court, one could right what was wronged. It was believed that this would empower the victims and thus facilitate their healing. When patients were encouraged by therapists to sue their supposedly sexually abusive parents, a group of defendants started what is called the False Memory Foundation.

The pendulum of societal reaction swung from one extreme to another. Suddenly, a number of aged parents were sued for having sexually abused their now adult children. This was followed by many of such cases being thrown out of courts as powerful experts/academics presented scientific evidence of how unreliable and malleable memory can be. They stated that recovered memory associated with therapy was even more highly suspect.

In fact, false memory syndrome has little relevance to the central issue of the phenomenon of DID. It is somewhat absurd to use false memory to discredit the diagnosis of DID. The central issue of DID is childhood trauma. How accurately the patient remembers the trauma has no relevance to the accuracy of the diagnosis.

We now know "false memory" can be induced by misguided therapists. Distressed patients, when they are seeking therapy, are in a vulnerable mental state. They are therefore indeed highly suggestible. When a therapist has a preconceived notion that childhood sexual abuse is frequently linked to anxiety and depression in adults, then the danger of implanting false memories of childhood sexual abuse to the patient would arise. This can be accomplished simply by the way questions are asked.

Indeed, at the height of this social trend of encouraging female clients to remember childhood abuse, many women were told by their therapists that "If you suspect that you have been sexually abused, then you must have been abused. If you do not remember sexual abuse, it is because you have repressed the memory." In other words, whether you remember or not, you were abused. This highly suggestive statement was taken as truth in some quarters.

Unfortunately, childhood sexual abuse is frequently associated with DID. If memory returns or is "recovered" in DID patients' therapy, the therapeutic focus is usually shifted to who did what to whom. This is a mistake. The therapeutic focus should be on the impact of the trauma on the patient's day to day functioning in the present.

It is true that if the therapist has their own agenda, memory "recovered" during therapy can be highly suspicious. However, that suspicion should be limited to the accuracy of the details of the abuse and not as to whether or not trauma has occurred. The trauma could have been physical, emotional or based on abandonment.

There is no doubt that memory can return out of the blue, after a car accident, or simply by watching a movie. This was true for many of my patients whose memory was triggered and returned after being buried for decades, but before they were in contact with any therapists.

Many critics assume that all recovered memories are false. Therapists have been accused of encouraging their patients to "remember" childhood abuse in order to promote ongoing therapy for the personal financial gain of the therapist. The voices in the academic debate became a cacophony. Some therapists were sued for misleading clients, and some DID patients recanted former charges of sexual abuse.

We have only to look at the shifting confabulations of our own memories to appreciate that we cannot retrieve indisputably accurate transcripts from our psyches about what happened in our past. There are many problems, from a psychotherapeutic point of view, with the launching of law suits and hurling of accusations about child abuse that is not corroborated by external evidence.[46] Seeking reparation through legal channels should be seen as very far from the essential task of therapy. The ultimate aim of therapy is healing, not revenge.

It is difficult to prove that abuse did or did not happen decades ago, particularly when there is only uncorroborated personal testimony to rely upon. With DID patients, questions about what is real in the inner world and what is real in the outer world are compounded. Genuine DID patients who uncover forgotten trauma could

---

[46]For further discussion of DID and the Law, see Engaging Multiple Personalities Volume 2 (publication pending)

easily recant their charges simply because the host does not hold these memories. Rather, they are held by an alter or several different dissociated fragments.

Similarly, an alter could be denying the experience of trauma because they are in control at the time of the statement and there remains an amnesic barrier blocking access to the traumatic memory. It is little wonder that so many psychiatrists shy away from DID patients. Because of the very nature of the patients' psychopathology, they are even more inconsistent in their self-reporting than the rest of us.

Dissociation, as a natural response to traumatic events, is the basis for many memory anomalies. Most psychiatrists today accept that traumatic memory operates differently than ordinary memory. It does not just fade and discolor with time and distance. It often falls through a trap door into darkness. Distressful memories that are contained and sealed up in a walled-off compartment is a hallmark of dissociation. Dissociation arises for the protection of the abused child in that way, and that amnesia can easily continue into adulthood.

This is a valuable lesson for therapists who are obsessed with learning the details of the original abuse. Going after such details is useless and harmful.

Joan (Chapter 1) came to see me primarily about the appearance of hazy memories of her early abuse. She thought she was losing her mind. She believed that the memories were delusions because she did not think that such abuse ever could have happened. The early abuse turned out to have indeed happened. She got better because she worked through and processed the past trauma, not because she relived the nightmares of her past for me.

False memory works both ways: There is also the possibility of "false negative memory." One should never underestimate the power of abusers' attempts to brainwash and influence a child victim. The simple question "Nothing ever happened to you. Are you sure you are not just dreaming?" or the chilling phrase, "No one will ever believe you." could be harrowing enough to silence an impressionable child for decades.

PTSD and DID

As far back as the end of the 19th Century, Pierre Janet[47] had observed that intense emotional reactions can cause memories of particular traumatic events to be dissociated from consciousness, and stored instead as visceral sensations such as bodily sensations of panic, or as visual images in nightmares and flashbacks. Janet observed that traumatized patients seemed to react to later cues reminiscent of that past trauma with the kinds of emergency responses that no longer were appropriate to the situation. In his recognition of the way that victims of trauma continue to be haunted, agitated, and provoked by later reminders of the trauma, Janet was way ahead of his time.

---

[47]Janet P, as described by van Der Kolk B A in Dissociation and the fragmentary nature of traumatic memories: Overview and exploratory study. Article first published online: 23 FEB 2006. DOI: 10.1002/jts.2490080402

Such victims cannot get past traumas that have scarred their psyches. Their energies are bound up with keeping their emotions under control rather than directly engaging with what is happening in the present. They may feel and behave as though they are continuing to be traumatized over and over again. Today, well over a century later, Janet's observations perfectly describe the post-traumatic stress syndrome (PTSD) associated with soldiers returning from the wars in Vietnam, the Persian Gulf, and Afghanistan as well as those who returned from World War I and II, with what was then termed "shell shock."

It is important to note that PTSD was not taken seriously until it was acknowledged as a "real" syndrome in 1980, the year when it was included in the official diagnostic manual, DSM-III. The high profile and articulate supporters of the military veterans from the Vietnam War had finally brought it to the attention of the world, and the condition could no longer be ignored or trivialized. Once acknowledged, the psychiatric community worked, as it continues to work, to develop treatment methods. Effective treatment methods are still being studied, developed and improved.

For abused children who have suffered severe trauma, there are no high profile and articulate supporters. These children have not been injured as a result of a war, with its consequent publicity, analysis, and support for soldiers who bravely served their country. Young, vulnerable children are always taught by their abusers, from the very beginning of abuse, that no one will believe them. Some of these children, even as they become adults, understand that no one really wants to know about childhood abuse or to recognize and acknowledge its terrible toll.

As noted earlier, DID is the result of repeated ongoing severe childhood trauma. In that sense, it is related to post-traumatic stress disorder (PTSD). The distinguishing characteristic is that the initial trauma happens before an integrated personality has fully developed, or is severe enough to split a still malleable personality. Further, the trauma is ongoing rather than a one-time event or short-term circumstance. Childhood abuse is the pernicious link from PTSD to DID.

Childhood Abuse

There is a general denial of the phenomenon of childhood abuse. This denial extends to its prevalence as well as its serious consequences in adult life; especially in the case of incest. Based on their clinical experience, many therapists, including myself, are convinced of the widespread nature of childhood sexual abuse.

It is difficult to provide convincing statistical evidence. At times, it is hard to agree on the definition of childhood physical, emotional and sexual abuse. It is also difficult to quantify the degree of trauma with respect to any specific traumatic event. Collecting statistics is hampered by denial, forgetfulness and actual pathological loss of memory through dissociation or repression.

Opponents often cite statistics indicating a percentage of early sexual abuse victims that did not develop pathology in later life as evidence minimizing the impact such abuse. Trauma does not happen in a vacuum. Analogously, it could be noted that only a percentage of population exposed to tubercle bacillus develop tuberculosis.

Many victims of childhood abuse grow up to be abusers themselves. It can be very significant if there is a protective cushion, such as a loving parent, who tries to set things right after the traumatic event. Alice Miller, in her book *"The Untouched Key"*, eloquently explained how tyrannical fathers produced diametrically opposite offspring like Paul Celan, the Romanian poet, and Adolf Hitler.[48] "Mother and aunts could come to Paul's aid and let him out of the closet when he was imprisoned (in the closet). These were the witnesses who rescued him, who helped him to understand that along with cruelty, rigidity and stupidity there can also be mercy and goodness and that he was not guilty and wicked but was even lovable, although his father hadn't noticed." On the other hand, Adolf Hitler, brutalized by his father, did not appear to have had any such protective cushion.

Through my clinical experience, I have come to the conclusion that early childhood abuse is common. Many victims are not as fortunate as Paul Celan to have a mother and aunts to soften the impact of the trauma. The effects of un-cushioned trauma in later adult life can be well hidden for decades within the survivor.

Part of the reason that so many experts in psychiatry do not believe in the diagnosis of DID may be linked to the denial of the breadth and impact of childhood sexual abuse.

---

[48]Alice Miller. The Untouched Key. 1990. Doubleday : New York, London, Toronto, Sidney, Auckland. P.56.

Harm from the continuous debate

Many patients presented in this book had the diagnosis of DID missed by their physicians and psychiatrists to the detriment of their well-being. Their dissociative symptoms were ignored or missed and the correct diagnosis was overlooked. They spent years going in and out of hospitals, or seeing different therapists. They were labeled as having bipolar disorder, treatment resistant depression, and/or the ubiquitous catch-all diagnosis of borderline personality disorder. They were incorrectly treated based on those diagnostic errors.

One cannot treat DID as something other than what it is, and expect recovery. Just as medications for pulmonary tuberculosis will not help a patient with heart failure, treatment for bipolar affective disorder will not help one suffering from DID.

Ruth (Chapter 5) was treated for a disease called "depression" with a course of ECT and numerous rounds of anti-depressants; Victoria (Chapter 7) was slated for ECT after failure to respond to anti-depressants, although the ECT was canceled at the last moment. In neither case was depression the disease. Rather, it was an appropriate emotion given their circumstances.

DID is officially and formally recognized in DSM 5. The ongoing failure to treat DID properly will continue, however, due to the fact that some psychiatrists from prestigious institutions still find the diagnosis controversial. Most untreated DID patients end up as chronic psychiatric invalids, going through repeated consultations with multiple therapists and hospital admissions. Without public awareness that the roots of DID lie in childhood abuse, education and prevention strategies cannot be implemented.

DID patients are as a significant group requiring our compassion and understanding. We can identify and treat DID more effectively once psychiatrists have developed a heightened awareness of trauma and dissociation, and de-emphasized the issue of so-called false memory, we can then treat DID more effectively.

This continuing controversy and debate has world-wide implications. DID is not confined to North America. Cultural attitudes may render DID, or at least reports of DID, invisible in some countries; just as wife-battering and child abuse are often ignored as a matter of cultural constraints. Nevertheless, it has been reported throughout the world, in such countries and cultures as diverse as Holland, Turkey[49], South Africa, China[50], Germany, and the Philippines[51].

---

[49]Akyüz G, Doğan O, Sar V, Yargiç LI, Tutkun H. Frequency of dissociative identity disorder in the general population in Turkey. Compr Psychiatry. 1999 Mar-Apr; 40(2):151-9.

[50]J.Yu and C.Ross. Dissociative Disorders Among Chinese Inpatients Diagnosed With Schizophrenia. J of Trauma Dissociation, 2010 July;11(3): 358-372.

[51]Gingrich H/D. Assessing Dissociative Symptoms and Dissociative Disorders in College Students in the Philippines. Journal of Aggression, Maltreatment & Trauma , 2009. vol. 18, no. 4, pp. 403-418.

Appendix 3 Reading List

1) Putnam, F. Diagnosis and Treatment of Multiple Personality Disorders. The Guildford Press. New York, NY. 1989.

2) Ross, C. Dissociative Identity Disorder. Second Edition. John Wiley & Sons, Inc., New York, NY. 1997.

3) Ross, C. The Osiris Complex: Case Studies in Multiple Personality Disorder. First Edition. University of Toronto Press, Scholarly Publishing Division. 1994.

4) Van der Kolk B.A. Psychological Trauma. American Psychiatric Press Inc. Washington. 1987.

5) Van der Kolk B.A. et al (editors). Traumatic Stress. The Guildford Press. New York. 1996.

6) Freyd J.J. Betrayal Trauma: The Logic of Forgetting Childhood Abuse. Harvard University Press. Cambridge, Massachusetts. 1996.

7) Barry M. Cohen et al (Editors). Multiple Personality Disorder from the Inside Out. The Sidran Press. Luthweville ,MD. 1991. Putnam's endorsement: "A helpful and hopeful look at another way of being; this book dispels the misleading stereotypes of MPD and illuminates the underlying human experience of this tragically misunderstood condition. A must for anyone whose life has been touched by this complex disorder."

8) Trujillo, O.R. The Sum of My Parts. New Harbinger Publications. Oakland, CA 2011.

9) Oxnam, R. B.   A Fractured Mind: My life with Multiple Personality Disorder. Hyperion, New York, NY. 2005.

Made in the USA
San Bernardino, CA
31 August 2014